Herbert Luck North

Arts and Crafts Architecture for Wales

ADAM VOELCKER

with a foreword by HRH The Prince of Wales

COMISIWN BRENHINOL HENEBION CYMRU

ROYAL COMMISSION
ON THE ANCIENT AND HISTORICAL MONUMENTS OF WALES

PUBLISHED IN ASSOCIATION WITH THE ROYAL SOCIETY OF ARCHITECTS IN WALES

ISBN 978-1-871184-41-9

British Library Cataloguing in Publication Data. A catalogue record for this book is available from the British Library
© Crown Copyright. RCAHMW 2011. All rights reserved. No part of this book may be reproduced, stored in a retrieval system or transmitted in any form or by any means, electronic, mechanical, photocopying, recording, scanning or otherwise, without permission from the publisher.

Comisiwn Brenhinol Henebion Cymru
Royal Commission on the Ancient and Historical Monuments of Wales

Crown Building, Plas Crug, Aberystwyth, Ceredigion, SY23 1NJ, United Kingdom

Telephone: 01970 621200   *e-mail:* nmr.wales@rcahmw.gov.uk   *Website:* www.rcahmw.gov.uk

ACKNOWLEDGEMENTS

All the images in this book are held in the National Monuments Record of Wales, with the exception of those belonging to the following individuals and organisations to whom we are grateful:

RIBA (Royal Institute of British Architects): pages 35, 67, 88
The Trustees of the Clough Williams-Ellis Foundation: pages 11 (bottom), 73
SPAB (Society for the Protection of Ancient Buildings): page 20
Patricia McGuire: page 37 (bottom)
Roger Haigh RIBA: page 37 (top)
English Heritage: pages 81, 83, 84
Pamela J. Phillips: pages 4, 10, 11, 12, 13, 14, 23, 68, 111

Most of the images have been created by the Royal Commission on the Ancient and Historical Monuments of Wales (Crown copyright). We have made best efforts to contact the copyright holders of other images. If we have failed to trace or acknowledge any copyright holder we would be glad to receive information to assist us.

Printed in Wales by: Cambrian Printers Limited

Contents

Foreword by HRH The Prince of Wales ... 5

Preface ... 7

Introduction ... 9

CHAPTER ONE
Early Life: 1871-1898 ...13

CHAPTER TWO
Early Projects: 1898-1900 ... 25

CHAPTER THREE
Domestic Work: 1900-1940 ... 39

CHAPTER FOUR
Church Work ... 75

CHAPTER FIVE
Other Work ... 103

CHAPTER SIX
North's Legacy ... 111

Notes and References ... 116

UK map ... 118

Chronological List of Selected Works ... 119

Herbert Luck North Collection ... 127

Bibliography ... 129

Index ... 131

Herbert Luck North 1871-1941

Foreword by HRH The Prince of Wales

CLARENCE HOUSE

Herbert Luck North was a romantic and a pragmatist. He loved the beauty and the simplicity of the humblest vernacular buildings of Wales, and he deeply appreciated their harmonious relationship with the landscape.

North was well ahead of his time in promoting what we have come to call 'local distinctiveness'. He might even be said to have developed the antecedents of design codes, noting over 100 years ago that "we should not break into the harmony of the landscape with something out of tune with the district", and drawing up guidelines for an appropriate palette of materials for new buildings in his parish of Llanfairfechan.

As a young man he worked in the office of Sir Edwin Lutyens. He seemed to have enjoyed success there, but he was a modest man whose heart was most in the humble buildings and landscape of North Wales. It was there that he lived most of his adult life and left his architectural legacy. This legacy is little known, although his buildings are much admired by those who know them.

This fascinating book will bring his work to a wider audience, and will hopefully lead to much greater appreciation of it. It is a tragedy that some of his most enchanting work has not survived, such as the extraordinary chapel at St. Winifred's Llanfairfechan, demolished despite protests from luminaries such as Sir John Betjeman.

This book's author, Adam Voelcker, is a natural heir to North, being a conservation architect whose home and office have long been in Snowdonia. North's work has inspired him, and I hope that this book will also inspire others to follow North's example of working creatively in a tradition rooted in its place.

Above all, with this book in hand, I can only encourage the reader to visit Herbert North's perfect garden village at Llanfairfechan in order to experience the harmony he always sought to achieve between new buildings and the land he loved.

Opposite. Portrait of North, c.1920s.

Courtesy of Pamela J. Phillips

Preface

I first became aware of Herbert Luck North about thirty years ago when driving around north Wales. Distinctive steep white gables, often a pair of them, would peep from behind a roadside hedge or perch on a hillside, and I knew an architect must be involved. Vernon Hughes, a locally-based architectural historian, told me that the architect was Herbert North. He put me in touch with Dr Ian Allan, who had written a doctoral thesis in 1988, which until now has been the only work about North, and through Ian Allan I met North's granddaughter, Mrs Pam Phillips. In 2006-9 I co-wrote the *Buildings of Wales* (Pevsner Architectural Guides) volume for Gwynedd. This provided an opportunity to see most of North's buildings in the region, but competition from castles, medieval churches and Victorian chapels inevitably prevented them from receiving the attention they deserved – and so the idea for this book was born.

Most of the available sources of information on North have been consulted during the course of my work. The Royal Commission on the Ancient and Historical Monuments of Wales holds at the National Monuments Record of Wales in Aberystwyth the Herbert L. North Collection, which includes an extensive range of original drawings and photographs covering the entire span of North's working life (see List, pages 127-8). Many of these are for schemes never executed, so they give an important insight into North's ideas. There are also photographs of buildings that have been altered or demolished.

Phil Thomas produced in 2000 a list of all known works by North, both built and unbuilt. This was compiled chiefly from a two-page list in North's own hand, giving the name or client of each project and the date. North's handwriting, however, is difficult to decipher in numerous instances, and at least thirty of the jobs are unidentifiable.

The most comprehensive source of information is Ian Allan's unpublished thesis. I have relied on this in no small part for many of the facts, and I am grateful to Mrs Mary Allan for lending me her copy. The background research for the thesis, including tapes of interviews (made when North's business partner, P. M. Padmore, was still alive), is also held by the Royal Commission, and this material has helped me to cross-check information where necessary.

During the course of my research I was contacted by Mary Sikkel and Harvey Lloyd who both happen to have collections of North's letters. These are interesting and useful, and it is hoped that the publication of this book may bring to light further original information.

Many others have given help, too, and I am grateful to them all: to Peter Burman for giving me the initial encouragement to embark on the book, and to Richard Suggett for suggesting that the Royal Commission might be interested in publishing it; to those who sent or helped retrieve vital information (Elaine Blackett-Ord, Frank Dann, Michael Drury, Karen Evans, Peter Jamieson, Lord Nickson, David Price, Frances Willmoth); to those who took photographs of buildings I was unable to visit (Iain Wright, Fiona Atkinson, Roger Haigh, Patricia McGuire, Frances Prior); to those who offered useful comments on my developing text (Simon Bradley, Susan Evans, Peter Howell, Penny Icke, Tom Lloyd, John Newman, Julian Orbach, Peter Wakelin, Eurwyn Wiliam, Chris Williams); to the Cambrian Archaeological Association, for giving me a grant to measure and draw the plans of some of North's buildings; and finally to all those owners or occupants of North buildings who kindly allowed me access to them.

Thanks are due, last but not least, to Pam Phillips, without whose help and encouragement this book would have been impossible. She allowed me access to her archives, which contain endearing letters written in Herbert's spidery handwriting when he was at school at Uppingham, many drawings and photographs, a series of seven scrapbooks in which North pasted pictures of buildings (and other things) that presumably took his fancy, and some of the architectural books in his library. She is also one of the few surviving people who remember North and has therefore been indispensable in the writing of the book.

Opposite. A typical North house in its setting (Neuadd Wen, The Close, Llanfairfechan).
RCAHMW, DS2011_092_001, NPRN 413201

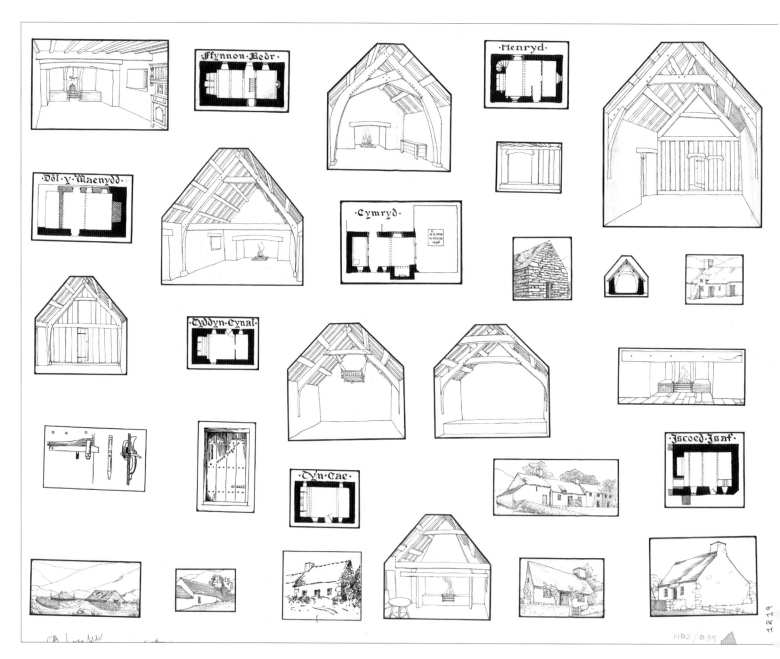

North's sketches of Snowdonian cottages, which he used to illustrate his book The Old Cottages of Snowdonia *(Hughes & North 1908).*
DI2010_0412

Introduction

This book is about a provincial architect who was not well known in Britain during his lifetime and who is even less known today, even in Wales, where he worked from 1901 until he died in 1941. Herbert Luck North is sometimes described as an Arts and Crafts architect, a label that places him conveniently in a recognisable category according to style and period. But, as with all labels, it does not tell the full story.

North's life began in the Victorian era and ended in the mid-twentieth century. He was the only child of a father and mother who were forty one and thirty six respectively when he was born in 1871. After his father died, when he was twelve, he spent much of his time in the company of his maternal grandfather. His outlook on life was therefore more mature than that of his contemporaries, even old-fashioned. When the world began to change and modernise after the calamitous First World War, North's heart belonged to the Edwardian period rather than the roaring twenties, probably remaining there for the rest of his life.

His position in architectural history places him in the last flowering of the Arts and Crafts movement. He was two generations younger than the movement's pioneers, people such as Philip Webb (1831-1915), Richard Norman Shaw (1831-1912) and John Dando Sedding (1838-1891). When North began his articles in London around 1893 it was a little too late to join the pupils of these architects on their sketching tours of the Continent. But he must have been aware of their travels and exploits when he joined Sedding's office, being run by Henry Wilson (1864-1934) since Sedding's death in 1891, and he would have known the organisations to which they belonged, such as the Art Workers' Guild and the Society for the Protection of Ancient Buildings (SPAB).

North was also slightly younger than these pupils – architects such as Edward S. Prior (1852-1932), William Lethaby (1857-1931), Ernest Gimson (1864-1919), Ernest Newton (1856-1922), Charles F. A. Voysey (1857-1941) and Charles R. Ashbee (1863-1942) – who formed the backbone

of the Arts and Crafts movement towards the end of the nineteenth century. Many of these younger architects were beginning to react against conventional architectural practice: some left for the country to become furniture makers; others became itinerant craftsmen-architects and travelled from job to job, often building with their own hands in the spirit of John Ruskin. North was at the tail-end of this exodus in 1895: while articled with Wilson he was sent to supervise the masonry work at Brithdir church, a gem of Arts and Crafts work in the heart of north Wales; and in the following year he was in charge of repairs at the Old Post Office at Tintagel on behalf of Detmar Blow (1867-1939) and the Society for the Protection of Ancient Buildings.

After returning to London and spending time in the young but already flourishing office of Edwin Landseer Lutyens (1869-1944), North left the metropolis for good and returned to Wales. His grandparents had moved to Llanfairfechan from Leicester in the 1850s, later followed by his parents, and when North returned there in 1901 it must have been the eventual prospects of money, family land and future clients that he had in his mind.[1] He did not establish a conventional office: he worked from a bedroom in his home at Wern Isaf, taking on the occasional assistant when he needed to, and a partner, P. M. Padmore, from 1926. His output was therefore not large, despite his prodigious energy.

This move to one of the remoter and poorer parts of Britain, while it gave him good local opportunities, probably prevented him from becoming better known. The quality of his early projects and competition successes demonstrates that he had a more than average ability, yet his clientele in north Wales was rarely of the wealthy, artistic sort whom architects such as Voysey, Lutyens and Baillie Scott had as patrons. With very few exceptions, North's houses were small.

His very early domestic projects were completed during his last years in London (described in Chapter 2). Between his return to Wales and the

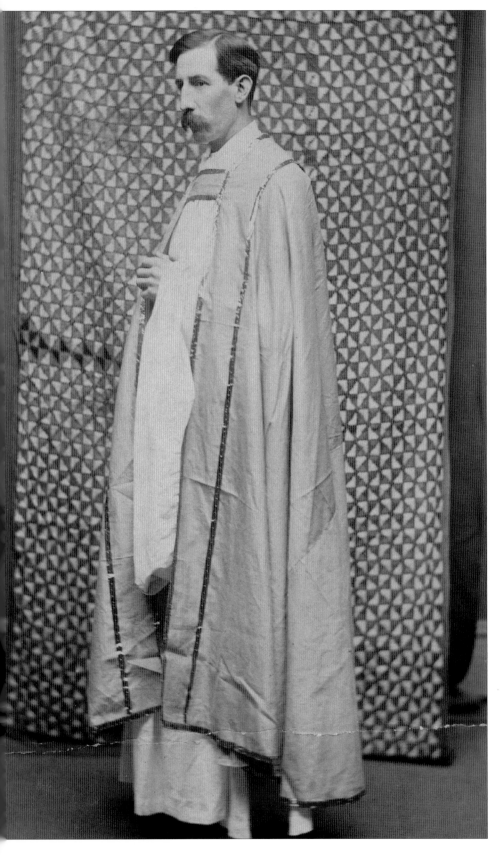

North in pageant costume, c.1910.

Courtesy of Pamela J. Phillips, DI2009_1385

beginning of the First World War he built a dozen houses, and it was during this period that he did his most interesting domestic work, weaving together fashionable Arts and Crafts ideas and features with those he was discovering in the local vernacular buildings of north Wales (Chapter 3). After the war and until his death he was continuously involved with developing family land in Llanfairfechan at The Close, an estate of small houses designed for individual clients. It is here that the quintessential North style is at its best: a hillside of picturesque white gabled cottages with roughcast walls, steep slate roofs and small-paned windows, each in its own garden bordered with beech hedges or traditional slate fences.

From a very early age North was deeply moved by ecclesiastical architecture, and though the opportunities to build new churches were far fewer than he would have wanted, he was always busy – and very content – designing fittings and schemes of decoration for existing churches (Chapter 4). Other non-domestic work included church halls, buildings for church schools and a small cottage hospital (Chapter 5). In his leisure hours he was often busy with church pageants: he produced them, wrote and designed the beautiful programmes (using the same Gothic script that he used to head his own letter-paper and in his books on the buildings of Snowdonia) and often acted in them; his wife was in charge of the music and the costumes. One can see how these pageants appealed to North: they enabled him to create his vision of the pre-modern world and to encapsulate its beauty and romance in gorgeous costume, scenery and music. The pageant provided a tiny model world in which North could be in total control.

North was a remarkable architect in the context of his north Wales contemporaries, primarily for his creation of a distinctive architecture suited to the region and his consistency of principles. This was in contrast to, for instance, G. A. Humphreys (1866-1948), who, as agent to the Mostyn estate, designed houses in and around Llandudno that were made of red brick and yellow sandstone, with red clay tiled roofs and half-timbered gables, the antithesis of North's approach. Sidney Colwyn Foulkes (1884-1971) also worked along the north

Glan Orme, Llandudno (G. A. Humphreys, 1897).

Adam Voelcker

landscape. One of Clough's earliest designs (unexecuted) was for a pair of labourers' cottages in north Wales, dated 1905. They are disarmingly simple, with white roughcast walls, a green slated roof and small cottage-casement windows, extraordinarily similar in spirit to some of North's contemporary designs.

North may have been outshone by the bravura and openness to new ideas of Clough Williams-Ellis, but there was a distinctiveness and a consistency to his work that distinguished him from Clough and their contemporaries and made his buildings so memorable. Beneath this aesthetic level there was also his passion for traditional buildings and a concern to find their relevance to modern building.

In a world that is growing more global by the day, yet is exhausting natural resources to the point that the collapse of society is not inconceivable, a return to 'small is beautiful' principles will surely become essential. Already, in planning legislation, policies encourage local distinctiveness in design, the use of local building materials, and small affordable homes that are economic to build and to maintain. It may be that in North's work, in addition to the aesthetic rewards, there are lessons to be learnt.

Portrait of North as a young boy, c.1876.

Courtesy of Pamela J. Phillips.
RCAHMW, DI2009_1388

coast, designing a wide variety of buildings, including houses, cinemas, hospitals, and civic, commercial and industrial buildings. North would not have liked Foulkes' eclectic approach to style, particularly his preference for the neo-Georgian, but the two men had much in common, including an interest in raising housing standards and a deep concern for the environment.

North's chief rival in any claim to fame is Clough Williams-Ellis (1883-1978). As people, North and Clough were poles apart. Richard Haslam has described Clough as 'individual, polymathic and cultured' and his work 'far-sighted and intelligent, human and uplifting, nourished at the springs of Classical tradition in Wales as well as Italy [...].'(Haslam 1996: 10). By Clough's own admission, he 'was born with a strange hankering, no less, for the spectacular, the showy and the grand.' (Williams-Ellis 1991: 32). He was physically well-built, had sartorial sense and was charming with people, whereas North was lean, socially shy and enjoyed colourful clothes only when they were pageant costumes. But they had much in common: a fascination with local buildings and vernacular styles, and a deep sympathy for the physical environment and the rooting of buildings in the

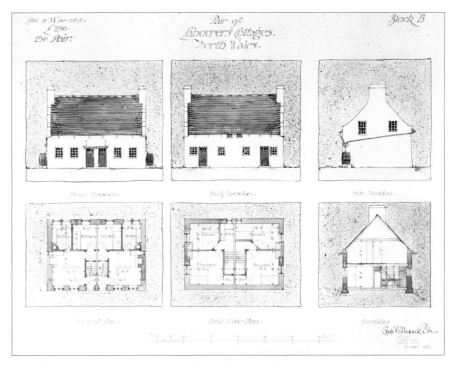

Pair of labourers' cottages, north Wales (Clough Williams-Ellis, 1905).

Courtesy of the Clough Williams-Ellis Foundation

Portrait of North as a young man, c.1893.

Courtesy of Pamela J. Phillips, DI2009_1384

Early Life: 1871-1898

Herbert Luck North was born on 9 November 1871 in Leicester, where his father, Thomas North, was a bank manager and a keen antiquarian.[2] Few records survive of Herbert's first decade but early photographs show a distinctive long nose and slightly wayward hair. His relationship with north Wales began early, as he used to holiday with his family in Llanfairfechan, on the north-facing coast of Caernarfonshire, staying with his mother's parents, Richard and Anne Luck. Richard Luck, a solicitor from Leicester, had moved to Llanfairfechan quite soon after buying land there from the Bulkeley estate in 1856. He continued working as a solicitor in north Wales and developed his new estate enthusiastically, building a house (Plas Llanfair) around 1863 and establishing a well-stocked farm and fruit orchard. As a result of his energy (and that of another newcomer, John Platt, an industrialist from Oldham), Llanfairfechan grew from a sleepy little village straddling its brook to a popular coastal resort linked to England by the Chester-Holyhead railway. Luck and Platt became village stalwarts; they were ardent churchmen and financed the new church, Christ Church, built in 1864.

The health of Anne Luck, Herbert's grandmother, was already poor when he was born. It seems that, when the Norths made their annual visit in 1881, she had deteriorated, because they stayed on and, in the autumn, Herbert began school there. Thomas North's health was not good either. He had contracted tuberculosis around the time of his son's birth and had retired with his family to Ventnor on the Isle of Wight in 1872.

In autumn 1883 Herbert began boarding at Uppingham School in Rutland. The first glimpses of his personality are recorded in a series of letters written over the next few years.[3] He liked – or said he liked – the school, yet he was always counting the days till he would be home again. He made friends easily enough. He liked drawing and singing, but not football ('it is such a rough game'). He was clearly able, and if he dropped in the half-term's order, he could pull himself up and come top by

Portrait of North as a schoolboy, c.1883.
Courtesy of Pamela J. Phillips, DI2009_1384

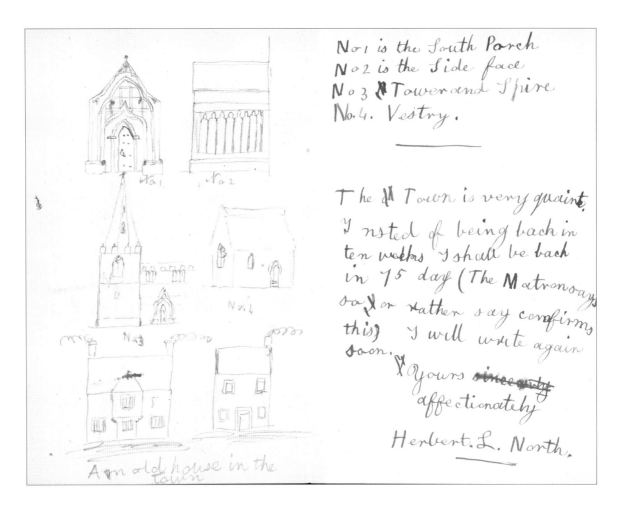

No 1 is the South Porch
No 2 is the Side face
No 3 Tower and Spire
No. 4. Vestry.

The Town is very quaint,
Ynsted of being back in
ten weeks I shall be back
in 75 day (The Matron says
so) or rather say confirms
this) I will write again
soon.
Yours ~~sincerely~~
affectionately

Herbert. L. North.

An old house in the town

A letter from North to his father, during his first term at Uppingham School, dated 6th October 1883. Note the methodical mind at work.

Courtesy of Pamela J. Phillips, DI2009_1389

the end of term. His conduct pleased the headmaster, who seems not to have been overly concerned by a stammer that obviously worried his father. The most telling remarks in the letters concern Herbert's growing interest in churches. Like William Morris when he was at Marlborough College (where he, too, hated rough games), North would go exploring churches whenever he had free time, and in his letters there are frequent requests for pens and rulers to draw sketches of his discoveries. His High Church upbringing is obvious too:

'I am sure that I should like to be a clergiman. The masters are rather low church here. One of them says that the Church of England began in the reighn of Henry VIII.'[4]

'I miss the Llanfairfechan service very much. I know where a come to be a cleargeman I shall have a different sort.'

The services at home were presided over by an Oxford-trained Ritualist, the Revd Philip Constable Ellis, whom the Bishop of Bangor had transferred to the fast-growing seaside resort in 1862 from Penmon, where he had repaired the friary church. He was to remain as rector until 1896 and would become well known to the North family.

In 1884, when Herbert was only 12, Thomas North died. Losing his father must have been a terrible shock for the boy. However, he gradually developed a relationship that filled some of the gap and was to prove of great significance to him during his teenage years: this was with a retired architect from Dudley, J. B. Davies, who settled in Llanfairfechan with his second wife. Davies had designed and repaired churches in the Dudley area and took a great interest in church and diocesan matters when he moved to north Wales. It was natural that Herbert found in him a sympathetic ear, a source of inspiration and a mentor. They wrote to each other regularly, and Herbert's letters reported on the churches he had found in the countryside around Uppingham, highlighting some of their finer features, even enclosing sketches. He asked Davies to set him an exercise to design a church, and it may have been Davies who gave him, in 1882, a copy of Bloxam's *Principles of Gothic Ecclesiastical Architecture*. By 1887 Herbert had been to London and seen J. L. Pearson's St John the Evangelist, Holborn (since demolished), for he wrote:

'I am afraid that I cannot write to you now about the London churches. Red Lion Square was lovely. But I shall be able to tell you better about it by word of mouth.'

Herbert went up to Jesus College, Cambridge in October 1890. A scrapbook made during this time contains two group photographs of him and his fellow-students but the majority are of architectural subjects: of his college (where the Pugin-restored chapel had William Morris decoration and Burne-Jones glass) and of a large number of churches he must have visited in Cambridgeshire and further afield, including Glasgow Cathedral, St Giles in Edinburgh and Melrose Abbey. There are also lithographs cut out of building journals, such as of G. E. Street's St John, Kennington (about which Herbert notes, 'How it speaks; almost Ideal'). Comments on other churches include 'fine' (Brooks' St Andrew, Plaistow), 'The Perfection' (St Mary, Beverley), 'unequalled in the World' (the west end of Peterborough Cathedral). Nearer home, St Mary, Betws-y-coed (by Paley & Austin, 1873) is 'Grand'. Against St John, Barmouth (Douglas & Fordham, 1889-98) he adds, more prosaically, 'clerestory'. His consuming passion for churches is quite clear and by this time he must have been sure about his vocation.

After gaining his degree at Cambridge in 1893 the next step was to find an office where he could take his articles.[5] Given his passion for churches, one assumes that his priority was for a good church practice, and a High Church one at that. But of those architects whose churches North must have admired, many were at the end of their working lives. By 1893 William Butterfield had almost run down his office, George Gilbert Scott, son of the 'Great Scott' and a convert to Catholicism from 1880, had gone mad, and John Dando Sedding had died in 1891. John Loughborough Pearson was completing his Catholic Apostolic Church in

Paddington, James Brooks had just completed churches at Gospel Oak and Hammersmith, and John Francis Bentley's great Westminster Cathedral was to begin in 1895.[6] Other possibilities for young architects included the offices of Richard Norman Shaw and Philip Webb. But Shaw was more known for his domestic work, and Webb never took on articled pupils, which ruled him out at this early stage of North's career (though it is

St John the Evangelist, Red Lion Square, London (J. L. Pearson, 1874-78) lithograph from The Building News, *3rd January 1879.*

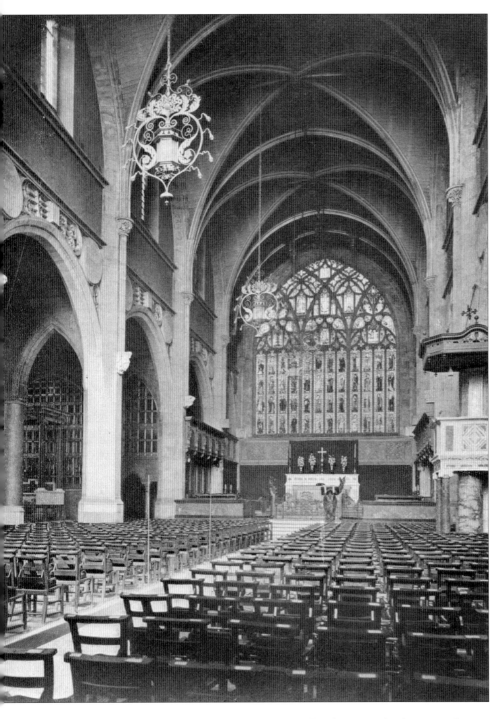

*Holy Trinity, Sloane Street,
London (J. D. Sedding, 1888-90).*

(Nicholson & Spooner c.1911)

'I think that there cannot be the slightest doubt that if Mr Sedding was alive, he would have been the man to have tried for. I am sure the more I think about that chapel at Welbeck[7] the more I feel his greatness. I never entered a building that had a quarter the human interest (at least certainly a new one); there was so much thought and sweet discursiveness in the little subject sculptures on the stalls bound together from subjects from the Benedicite, and so much outdoor feeling in the decorative work, that it felt like Chaucer [...]. Well even if Mr Wilson is not a genius, still it would be something to live with a man who cannot have failed to catch some of the spirit, and who has I expect the same connexion as Mr Sedding.'

Sedding was a passionate Anglo-Catholic and believed that the beautified altar was the true centre of Christian worship and more important than the building that contained it. This had two effects. One was to elevate the altar and church fittings generally to works of art and craftsmanship. The other effect was to play down the importance of architectural style, that is the Gothic style, in an attempt to replace it with a new style more fit for Anglo-Catholic ceremonial. He wanted churches to be 'by living men for living men', and in this pursuit he was a true exponent of Arts and Crafts philosophy. 'The real architect of a building ... must be his own clerk of works, his own carver, his own director, he must be the familiar spirit of the structure as it rises from the ground ... to make the most of the site and the building applied to it.' (Drury 2000: 85)

North clearly admired Sedding but appeared indifferent to Wilson in his letter. This may be because he did not yet appreciate the importance of Wilson's role. He loved Sedding's chapel at Welbeck Abbey without perhaps realising that Wilson was behind the tour de force of craftsmanship displayed in the building. In 1890 Wilson had also completed Holy Trinity, Sloane Street, another remarkable display of Arts and Crafts work, and St Peter, Ealing, was being completed around 1893, just as North joined the office. The Church of Our Holy Redeemer, Clerkenwell, designed in 1887-8, was completed by Wilson in 1895 (its tower was added in 1906).

The atmosphere of the office when North joined was perhaps of an Arts and Crafts studio as much

tempting to speculate how North's future might have developed had he joined Webb, for the two men were very similar in temperament and practice).

In the event North chose Sedding's office, now run by Henry Wilson. Some clues as to his reason for choosing this practice are revealed in a letter he wrote to Davies before leaving Cambridge:

St Mark, Brithdir,
(Henry Wilson, 1895-98).
RCAHMW, DS2010_001_001,
NPRN 43883

as of a traditional architectural practice. The philosophy of 'hands-on' involvement in the building process was fundamental to Sedding, who had learned this from his teacher, G. E. Street (also William Morris's teacher). When he said the architect must be his own carver, he meant it: while he was looking after the building of St Clement, Bournemouth, he used to spend the evenings in his lodgings carving pieces of stone (MacCarthy 1994: 107). Sedding's Arts and Crafts approach attracted young men who were later well-known as architect-craftsmen. Alfred Powell (1865-1960, also from Uppingham), Ernest Gimson (1864-1919, also from a wealthy Leicester family) and Ernest Barnsley (1861-1926) all passed through his office in the late 1880s and were about to set up their homes and workshops in the Cotswolds. Arthur Grove (1870-1929) was in the office when North joined; he subsequently worked with E. S. Prior

and later carried out church work mostly in Wales. So was Charles Quennell (1872-1935), an outstanding student, later an architect of suburban and country houses in Hampstead Garden Suburb and the Home Counties, and perhaps best known for his *History of Everyday Things in England* (1918). North may have coincided with Charles Nicholson (1867-1949), who left sometime in 1893 and later became an important church architect. Detmar Blow had probably been working for Sedding around 1890 and was still in the old office in Oxford Street working on his own jobs. He was another of the itinerant architect-craftsmen inspired by Ruskin and Morris, who, in the first half of his life, travelled around Britain building with his own hands (Drury 2000).

It is not known exactly what North did in Wilson's office during the first year or two of his articles. Considering the maturity of the drawings

of churches he had made when he was at school, he probably arrived well equipped to meet the challenges Wilson set him. North must have progressed rapidly because, in 1895, Wilson sent him back to north Wales to supervise the building of Brithdir church, near Dolgellau. It is not entirely clear how Wilson got the commission to design this remarkable church; it may have come through Sedding's circle of High Church friends. His client was Mrs Louisa Tooth, who wished to build a church in memory of her second husband, the Revd Charles Tooth, former chaplain of St Mark's English Church in Florence.[8] The convenience of sending North back to Wales was obvious and Wilson explained to Mrs Tooth that this would reduce the need for and cost of his own visits. He put North in charge of the masonry work; for the carpentry he sent Charles Quennell. Arthur Grove shared with Wilson the running of the job from London and both men had a hand in making some of the fittings (Grove the lead font, Wilson the copper-faced altar and pulpit). The contract, which was not completed until 1898, was a fraught one.

The surviving letters between Wilson and Mrs Tooth indicate an awkward and demanding client, and an architect who preferred designing buildings and making fittings to organising building sites and wayward builders, who were accustomed to doing things in their own way (Allan 1979 and 1980). The masonry, in particular, caused Wilson considerable concern. He wanted the granite blocks to be random and undressed so that the church looked as if it had grown out of the mountainside, but the mason could not be persuaded to do 'rough' work. North must have been involved in this battle, for Wilson wrote to Mrs Tooth in December 1895:

'that North should fluster the men rather surprises me because he tries to be so clear. I thought he was getting on so well. He certainly sends very good accounts of the masons and masonry.' (Allan 1979: 289)

However, when Wilson visited the site in early 1896 he found the masonry 'being too carefully done.' Perhaps North himself was becoming too

Above. Carving on Spanish walnut choir stall. St Mark, Brithdir.
RCAHMW, DS2007_228_016

Above, left. Nave doors, inlaid with teak, ebony and mother-of-pearl. St Mark, Brithdir.
RCAHMW, DS2007_228_003

Opposite page. Interior of St Mark, Brithdir (Henry Wilson, 1895-98).
RCAHMW, DS2007_228_005, NPRN 43883

flustered, because he seems to vanish from the scene (Grove and Quennell stayed), next appearing in Cornwall later in the year. Did he ask to be removed from an uncomfortable situation or did Wilson take him away? North's granddaughter remembers him getting very upset when things went wrong even in his later years; for a young and inexperienced architect the situation must have been highly challenging. Perhaps an informal leave of absence was how North's first real job ended.

The Cornwall posting came about through Detmar Blow. In 1895 the Society for the Protection of Ancient Buildings (SPAB) was alerted to the threatened demolition of a medieval manor-house, the Old Post Office at Tintagel. Thackeray Turner, its secretary, asked Detmar Blow to go down to rescue the building. Blow agreed, but in the event he was too busy with other jobs and recommended that North go in his place. A further reason why Blow could not be in Tintagel was because William

Morris was dying. Indeed, Blow was beside Morris's bed when he died on 6 October 1896. This must have been a poignant moment for North, for whom Morris had been, and would always be, a great inspiration.

North seems to have been put in charge of the repair work, organising the workmen and paying them from funds that Turner was raising from the SPAB office. North sent him progress reports with his requests for money. The work was

'being done with the greatest care and we save all that it is possible to save and I think it no small thing if we can do anything which shall remind people of the beautiful simplicity of life of their ancestors.'[9]

North might subsequently have gone in the same direction that a number of SPAB-associated architects went: people like William Weir (1865-

The Old Post Office, Tintagel. North was in charge of repair work here in 1896, on behalf of Detmar Blow and SPAB.

Courtesy of SPAB

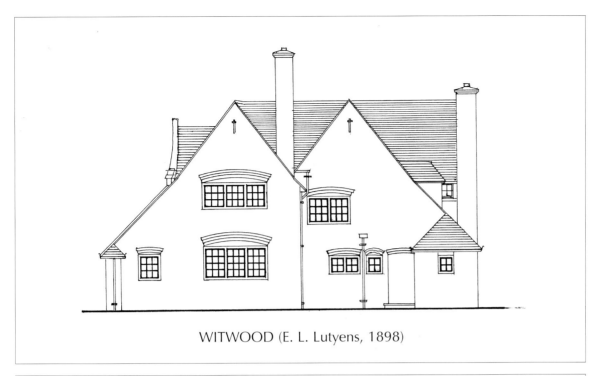

WITWOOD (E. L. Lutyens, 1898)

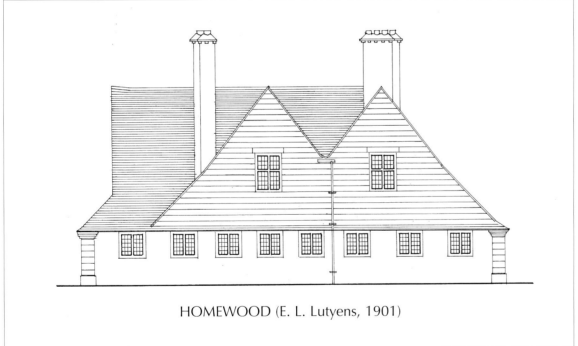

HOMEWOOD (E. L. Lutyens, 1901)

Two houses by Lutyens, probably designed during North's time in Lutyens' office around 1896-97.

RCAHMW, (top) DI2010_0425, (left) DI2010_0426, Adam Voelcker

1950), who travelled around the country repairing old buildings in the careful, minimal way advocated by Morris; but North did not even become a member of SPAB, then or later. Alongside his passion for old buildings – which bore fruit a few years later when he wrote two pioneering books about the old churches and cottages of Snowdonia – there was a creative streak in him which the repair of old buildings could not satisfy. In a letter of 1913 to the Llandudno architect, G. A. Humphreys, he wrote 'To be candid I far prefer new buildings to old and am not at all ashamed of it'. It was perhaps a recognition of this that prompted his next move, in late 1896 or early 1897, to the office of Edwin Lutyens, who was his senior by only two years but was already developing a great reputation.

There is a story that, when North went for interview, Lutyens took him on immediately because he liked North's shoes – stout working-men's boots, proving the Arts and Crafts credentials of an architect well used to being on site with the builders. Lutyens had set up office around 1889 when he was 20, and at the time North joined him he was busy designing Munstead Wood for Gertrude Jekyll. It is not certain exactly how long North stayed but, assuming it was for a year or two, he would have seen an impressive list of house commissions develop on Lutyens' drawing-board. The Orchards and Witwood were built in 1898; Overstrand Hall, Tigbourne Court and Goddards, all in 1899; Deanery Garden, Marsh Court and Homewood in 1901. The office must have had a heady atmosphere in these early days, with every promise of future success for Lutyens with his precocious talents and his growing high society connections (he married Lady Emily Lytton in 1897), but one doubts that North was entirely at ease helping design houses for the rich when his heart was with churches and humbler buildings. On a superficial level he picked up (or dare one suggest he helped develop?) ideas of formal composition. A brief look at the drawings of Witwood and Homewood instantly reminds one of typical North houses built soon afterwards. Socially, he shared the company of like-minded assistants, some of whom remained lifelong friends: Robert Marchant, who helped North with his book on Welsh churches and later practised in Kent; W. H. Ward, who designed houses in Hampstead Garden Suburb and the Lake District, was chairman of the Church Crafts League and wrote

books on French architecture; and O. M. Ayrton, who went into partnership with J. W. Simpson and specialised in concrete construction. The house designs of Marchant and Ward show an uncanny similarity to North's, perhaps the result of a common inheritance from their time with Lutyens.

The precise date of North's departure from Lutyens's office is not known. According to P. M. Padmore, North's partner from 1926, there was a furious 'bust-up' at Lutyens' office and the four assistants walked out.[10] North and his three colleagues shared a house at 2 Bedford Square and were joined by F. C. Eden, W. G. St J. Cogswell, A. Durst and J. S. Lee. There is no evidence that this group worked as a professional partnership on joint projects; it was more like a Morris brotherhood of kindred spirits. During or after this episode, around 1899, North worked for W. A. Pite (with whom Ayrton had worked in 1897), brother of Beresford Pite, church architect and later a specialist in the design of hospitals.[11]

By now, North was already working on designs for his first projects in north Wales, so his intention was clearly to leave the metropolis and to return to his adopted home in Snowdonia. In 1897 he had married Ida Maude, the daughter of his mentor and surrogate father, J. B. Davies. Ida had trained as a pianist at the Royal College of Music in London. They set up home at 10 Yew Grove, Cricklewood, and their only child, Ida Joan, was born in 1898. Richard Luck, North's grandfather, died in the same year, leaving his daughter Fanny (North's mother) to look after the estate. North and his wife must have felt a duty to look after two ageing widows: Fanny (now 63) and Ida's step-mother.[12] Besides, Richard Luck and Thomas North had left their estates in trust to Herbert, so returning to north Wales made much sense. Land, money and clients looked secure, even if not on Lutyens' scale.

*Portrait of Ida Maude North
(née Davies), c.1897.*

*Courtesy of Pamela J. Phillips,
DI2009_1383*

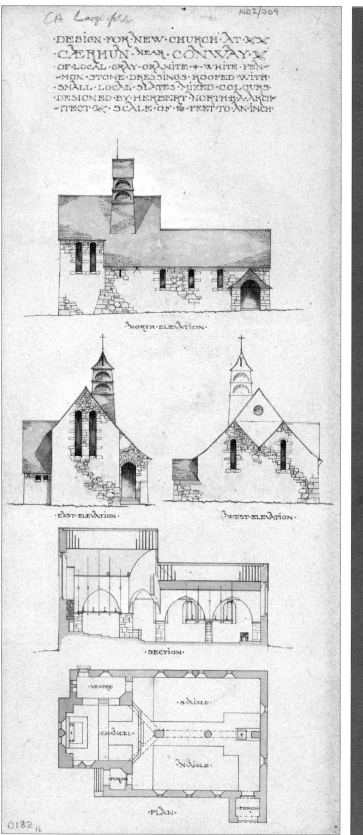

DESIGN·FOR·NEW·CHURCH·AT
CÆRHUN·NEAR·CONWAY
OF·LOCAL·GRAY·GRANITE·+·WHITE·PEN-
MON·STONE·DRESSINGS·ROOFED·WITH
SMALL·LOCAL·SLATES·MIXED·COLOURS
DESIGNED·BY·HERBERT·NORTH·BA·ARCH-
ITECT·&·SCALE·OF·16·FEET·TO·AN·INCH

NORTH·ELEVATION.

EAST·ELEVATION.   WEST·ELEVATION.

SECTION.

VESTRY   S·AISLE

CHANCEL

N·AISLE

PORCH   PORCH

PLAN.

0182 16

BUILDER'S
JOURNAL
COMPETITION
FOR·HOUSE
NEAR·HYTHE
FIRST

PREMIATED
DESIGN
IN·BRICK
ROUGHCAST
BOARDING
·+·THATCH

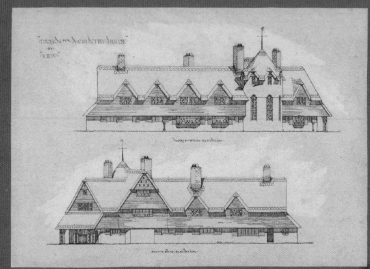

DESIGN·FOR·A·COUNTRY·HOUSE
"YEW"

NORTH·WEST·ELEVATION.

SOUTH·EAST·ELEVATION.

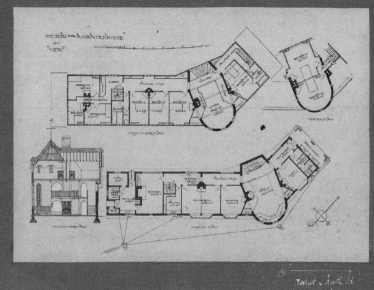

DESIGN·FOR·A·COUNTRY·HOUSE
"YEW"

Early Projects: 1898-1900

One of North's first Welsh projects, carried out while he was still in London, was for a new church at Caerhun in the Conwy valley. The date of the design is about 1898, but it was never built.[13] The interest of this scheme is in North's response to the setting. It was to be a rough country church, built of the local stone and slate, irregular in form – organic almost, as if it had stood for centuries. The drawings suggest a pleasing formal progression as the roof-lines step from porch to nave roof, then slide up over the chancel and finally reach a climax with the two-tier arcaded bellcote. Admirers have commented on how Welsh the church looks,

but it is not Welsh at all. It is hardly like the Conwy valley churches, least of all with its curious bellcote, which is surely Alpine. Nevertheless, North was responding to the poetry of the setting in the way he had learned from Wilson at Brithdir church (completed the same year, 1898), and possibly from another church not so far away at Caerdeon, where the Revd J. L. Petit had built something equally foreign but at the same time entirely appropriate to its mountain setting in 1862. Less convincing in North's design is the bizarre plan: a pair of naves (a feature of local churches in the Conwy valley) share the same central chancel,

Opposite. Design for a new church at Caerhun (1898); and opposite right, competition entry for a house near Hythe (1899).
RCAHMW, DI2010_0404 and DI2008_1252

St Philip, Caerdeon, (designed by Revd J. L. Petit, 1862).
RCAHMW, DS2010_663_001

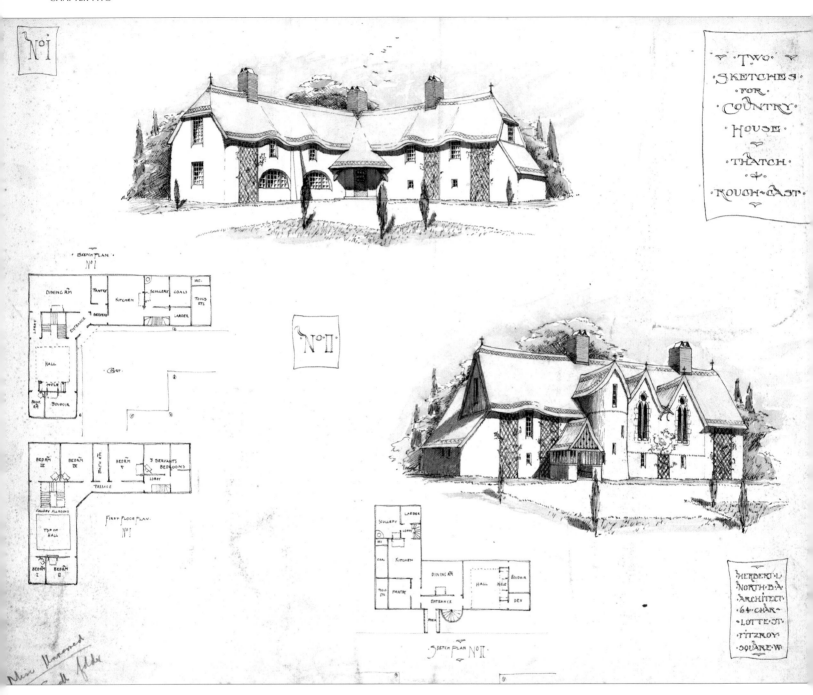

Designs for two thatched country houses (probably c.1898).

RCAHMW, DI2008_1277

the junction formed by a pair of chancel arches set at 45 degrees on plan, and backlit from the west by a high-level window above the central valley.

Of the half dozen projects that North designed at this time, while he was still in London, only two were not for buildings in Wales. The first was for two country houses for an unspecified site (presumably not in Wales, as the roofs were thatched). There is no suggestion that they were ever built. They were L-shaped in plan, with the domestic services in one wing and the reception rooms in the other. The defining feature of both was a double-height hall with fireplace inglenook and a three- or four-sided gallery. The style of each was decidedly picturesque, with the thatch gently lifting over the upper windows like eyebrows. One of the houses had a projecting semicircular stair turret and, next to it, a pair of gables lighting the double-height hall through tall, pointed lancets like church windows.

The country house, again, was the theme of North's next project, submitted under the name 'Yew' for a competition run by *The Builders' Journal* in May 1899. This was for a real site near Hythe in Kent and for a real client (an unnamed reader of the journal), and a real brief had been prepared. Indeed, there was every chance that the winner would be commissioned. 'I want a house long and low,' the client requested, 'a large square entrance hall, to be used as a comfortable sitting-room, a wide staircase, and a gallery going partly round hall, a dining-room and boudoir for a lady, about six bedrooms, and three servants' rooms, with comfortable offices etc. I want something a little unusual, either dark stained wood and thatch, or old timbers and thatch, and all kinds of angles and windows.' The brief was taken up by an enormous number of competitors: 134 entries were received and exhibited for a week at the Architectural Association. E. S. Prior was the assessor. He chose North as the winner, awarding him twenty guineas.

North's entry followed the requirements of the brief conscientiously. In essence the plan was one of the favourite Arts and Crafts arrangements: a single bank of rooms facing the views, with a linking corridor behind. The client was given his long house; but North relieved its attenuated footprint by bending it, so that two low arms, a short and a long, radiated from a double-height hall in a taller hub. It was almost a butterfly plan, another *parti* popular at the time for reasons of aesthetic formality as well as providing views and trapping the sun. R. Norman Shaw's remodelling of Chesters, Northumberland in 1891 may have been the first example; others include Happisburgh Manor, Norfolk, by Detmar Blow and Ernest Gimson (1900), Baillie Scott's (unexecuted) House for an Art Lover (1901) and Lutyens' Papillon Hall, Leicestershire (1902).[14] North's plan must have appealed to Prior, who had used the butterfly plan himself at The Barn, Exmouth (1896-7), and later at Home Place, Norfolk (1904-6). The progression from entrance porch to entrance hall, then into the rear of the great hall, was dramatic and well handled. The hall had a bowed garden front with three tall windows rising through both storeys, a

nook with a tiny window on each side, and a gallery running around three sides of the hall. The roof was thatched, with prominent gabled dormers breaking through the deep eaves, and a dovecote in the main gable at the rear of the great hall. The upper storey was weather-boarded and tarred, jettied out above a white roughcast ground storey with leaded windows and cabbage-green shutters.

The house was quite unlike any other that North was to design. It had a romantic, picturesque feel, in the vein of Arts and Crafts houses in Kent and Surrey, or the thatched houses that Ernest Gimson and Alfred Powell were building in the Cotswolds at this time. North was clearly respectful of the local vernacular in a way that some of his more famous contemporaries, such as Voysey, rarely were. The house would have been larger than any other he designed (except for Keldwith, pages 45-9) and the size gave him the freedom to play with the spaces in a way he rarely could elsewhere. The great hall here would have been worthy of Baillie Scott in the drama of its double-height space. Sadly, North collected only the prize money, and he was not commissioned to build the house he had designed.[15] It is tantalising to wonder how North's career would have developed if this project had been completed or if he had remained in southern England, with its greater numbers of wealthy clients and opportunities for large-scale commissions.

In the same year North designed a lodge for R. Norton at Penrhiwardir, Tal-y-cafn, Flintshire. The drawings show North still in his early picturesque style: they present a sort of secular equivalent to the Caerhun church, with rough stone walls, steep slated roofs, a round-headed window and door, a semicircular stair tower with conical roof, and a big pointed archway with battered base walls. The scheme was published in *The Builders' Journal* in December 1899 but it remained unbuilt until 1928, when the same design seems to have been executed for a new client.

Finding the implementation of his designs constantly thwarted must have been frustrating for North. His first success in bringing designs to fruition and being able to demonstrate his capabilities came when he began to develop land owned by his family at Llanfairfechan. Bolnhurst and Northcot were individual commissions for houses, built around 1898-9 at the bottom of what would later become The Close. Northcot looks to

Estate house by George Benmore, architect to North's grandfather. Compare the low porch roof here and on page 55.

Adam Voelcker

Northcot, Llanfairfechan (1899). Almost all of North's buildings were roughcast; this house is a notable exception.

RCAHMW. DS2010_660_001, NPRN 409680

Arch to inglenook, Bolnhurst, Llanfairfechan (1898).

Adam Voelcker, NPRN 406858

be the earlier in the development of North's ideas, though it may post-date Bolnhurst in construction. Its walls are of exposed stone, not roughcast like almost all his later buildings; the windows are vertical sliding sashes, not the cottage-casement type he later used; the roofs have timber barge-boards, not plain slated verges. The character is more akin to the sort of Victorian gabled house that Richard Luck, his grandfather, had commissioned for himself from George Benmore,[16] a local architect who had worked under the Diocesan Surveyor, Henry Kennedy, and later designed buildings for the Penrhyn estate around Bangor. The rooms open off the double-height hall; the staircase rises towards the rear wall, then divides both ways to give access to the gallery, which returns round the space on three sides. The detail is kept plain and simple, letting the space speak for itself. The only unsatisfactory element is the central pier, which interrupts the axis between front door and staircase.

The plan of Bolnhurst is an L, with the entrance in the internal angle, the drawing room and the dining room either side of the entrance hall, and the kitchen at the external angle. The most attractive feature is the lean-to inglenook which grows out from the drawing room gable. Internally

it has a tiled fireplace, a tiny window and a pointed gothic archway connecting the nook to the main room – this is an early use of the sort of pointed arch that became typical of North, with a very low spring-line and barely curving heads. The stone walls are roughcast; the roof is slated with small random slates. The rear chimney is diagonal on plan, reflecting the diagonally placed fireplace in the corner of the dining room, and perhaps a

Plan of Northcot.

DR = Drawing room, St = Study, H = Hall, D = Dining room, K = Kitchen

Adam Voelcker, DI2010_0418, NPRN 409680

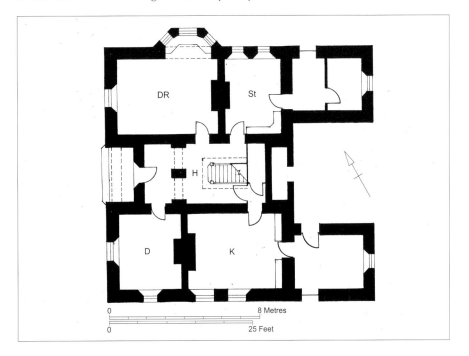

Opposite page. Lodge at Tal-y-cafn (designed 1899, built 1928).

Adam Voelcker

Bolnhurst, Llanfairfechan (1898).
RCAHMW, DS2007_402_001, NPRN 406858

Bedroom at Wern Isaf.
RCAHMW, DS2010_076_038, NPRN 301624

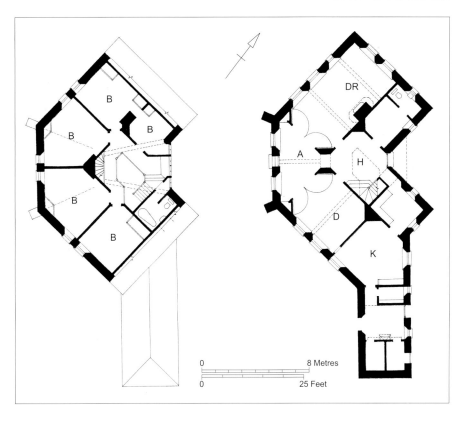

nod to medieval Welsh houses where a diagonal chimney stack was sometimes used to show gentry status. Some distinctive features from his earlier house designs appear in Bolnhurst that North tended to avoid in subsequent buildings: eyebrow dormers and rounded heads to doorways and windows. From this point onwards he preferred angles to curves, his buildings becoming less picturesquely pretty and more severe, almost modernist in their starkness.

A case in point is his next house, Wern Isaf at Penmaen Park, Llanfairfechan,[17] an early masterpiece which he designed for himself and Ida when they left London for good in May 1901. The only curves here are in the gently pointed heads to the main doorways.[18] The plan is based on a tight geometry of diagonals. The entrance is into an octagonal hall around which the rooms radiate on both storeys, the three main reception rooms facing out west, at 45 degrees to each other, looking towards the Menai Strait and Anglesey. The three main rooms are interconnected to form a continuous space, being separated by large glazed doors which swing back fully against lengths of wall sized to contain them. The result is a complex interplay of spaces, new in North's career and certainly new to north Wales. A local newspaper, announcing North's success in the Country House competition, also mentioned his new house:

'At the present moment a large house is in course of erection on the Plas estate, Llanfairfechan from Mr North's plans, and it can be safely said that there is not such another in the neighbourhood showing such originality, and at the same time so pleasing a sight to lovers of architecture.'[19]

There are other complexities. The three elevations facing the views consist of three steep gables, each with a pair of tall narrow windows to the bedrooms. Each bedroom appears from the outside to fit snugly into its own gable, but in fact the rooms span across the valleys and the paired windows sit either side of the dividing partitions. The result is unexpected yet subtle and produces enchanting bedroom spaces. The octagonal hall is an intriguing space, too. The stair winds up around three sides of the octagon, then the landing gallery continues round to complete the circle. It feels tight and cramped, however, as if a grand idea has been forced into a house too small for it. Perhaps the spacious Hythe plan was still in North's mind.

Perhaps not surprisingly there is at Wern Isaf something of the spirit of Red House, the house that Webb designed for William Morris at Bexleyheath in 1859. The exterior may be more controlled and symmetrical than at Red House, and lacks its Ruskinian 'changefulness', but the steep roof and the pointed arch of Webb's entrance porch must surely have influenced North. Internally, too, there is much that recalls Morris's house: the simple plainness of the walls contrasting with the honestly expressed details (always kept to

Plans of Wern Isaf, Llanfairfechan (1900).

B = Bedroom, DR = Drawing room, A = Ante-room, H = Hall, D = Dining room, K = Kitchen

Adam Voelcker, DI2010_0429, NPRN 301624

the minimum), the built-in and painted dressers and cupboards, the exposed beams and, of course, the Morris embroideries.[20]

North also designed the garden at Wern Isaf (just as Webb had designed the garden at Red House).

His love of gardens and gardening had probably been instilled by his grandfather, Richard Luck, a keen gardener and fruit-grower, who had often enjoyed Herbert's help in the orchards at Plas Llanfair. The garden at Wern Isaf was conceived as

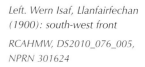

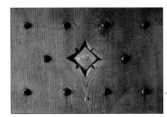

Wern Isaf: prism in front door.
RCAHMW, DS2010_076_009,
NPRN 301624

Right. Wern Isaf: drawing room.
RCAHMW, DS2010_076_032,
NPRN 301624

Below. Wern Isaf: view from
drawing room through ante
room to dining room.
RCAHMW, DS2010_076_025,
NPRN 301624

an extension of the house, with terraces arranged concentrically around the radiating plan, the changes of level defined by low dry-stone walls or hedges. The planting becomes increasingly natural in each successive terrace, so that, at the perimeter of the garden, it is more woodlands than garden. An oak tree stands on the small island formed within a turning-circle outside the front door; a diagonal axis passes from the oak through the centre of the house to a pool and runnel disappearing into the undergrowth. This axis passes through a tiny prism set into the front door, a feature repeated at other houses. Was it just whimsy on North's part, or did he, like Lethaby, have a genuine belief in the mysterious forces of energy?

For North it must have been a decisive step to design his own house. Without a client he was free from extraneous constraints; on the other hand, it was an opportunity, a duty perhaps, to put his beliefs into practice – a more demanding challenge for some architects, who are their own sternest critics. One certainly feels that Wern Isaf was intensely designed.

North's passionate interest in buildings suggests that he would have been aware of other notable houses being built during his time in London at the very end of the nineteenth century. 1898 was the

Stoneywell Cottage, Ulverscroft (designed by Ernest Gimson, built by Detmar Blow, 1899).

Copyright RIBA Library Photographs Collection

The Barn, Exmouth (designed by E. S. Prior, 1896-97).

Copyright RIBA Library Photographs Collection

year that Ernest Gimson's stone and thatched Stoneywell Cottage (at Ulverscroft, Leicestershire) was built by Detmar Blow. The house looked as if it had grown out of the rocks on which it sat, 'Arts and Crafts at its most earthy' (Davey 1995:163). Alfred Powell, also from Sedding's office, designed Long Copse (at Ewhurst, Surrey) at about the same time, also thatched. E. S. Prior's The Barn at Exmouth (1896) was a good example of the butterfly plan, developed from a cottage project published in *The British Architect* in May 1895. In 1900 Ernest Gimson and Detmar Blow built their version of the butterfly plan, Happisburgh Manor, in Norfolk. In all these, we see a link with North's Hythe competition, and then a progression to Wern Isaf which is itself a variation of the butterfly plan adapted to its site orientation.

Other influences on North were the work of

Butterfly-plan houses.

Adam Voelcker, DI2010, 0848

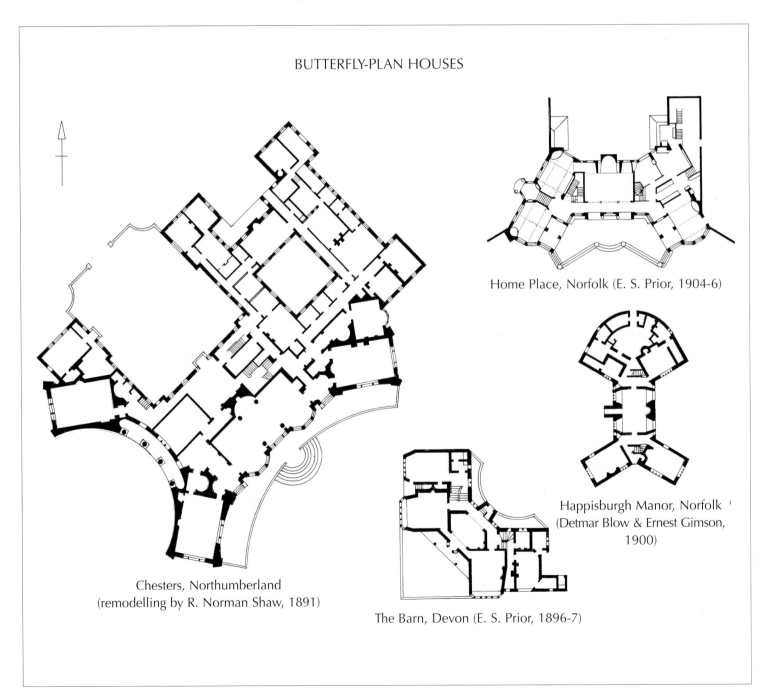

BUTTERFLY-PLAN HOUSES

Home Place, Norfolk (E. S. Prior, 1904-6)

Happisburgh Manor, Norfolk
(Detmar Blow & Ernest Gimson, 1900)

The Barn, Devon (E. S. Prior, 1896-7)

Chesters, Northumberland
(remodelling by R. Norman Shaw, 1891)

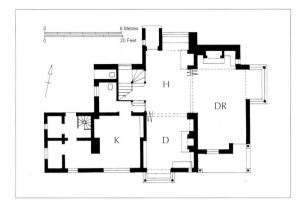

Plan of Red House, Douglas (M. H. Baillie Scott, 1912-13).
K = Kitchen, H = Hall, D = Dining room, DR = Drawing room
Adam Voelcker, DI2010_0734

Baillie Scott and Voysey. Baillie Scott had been displaying his houses in *The Studio* from 1893, and in other contemporary magazines, as had Voysey. Around 1896-7 Baillie Scott was moving from his early half-timbered style to a plainer, more severe one, a move that Voysey had made earlier. More importantly, Baillie Scott was exploring ways of replanning smaller houses so that the interior spaces intermingled, flowing vertically as well as horizontally, with the hall (he called it the 'house-place') always the focus. North certainly borrowed these new ideas. The double-height hall was used in his Hythe competition design and his two thatched house designs, and the interconnecting rooms in Wern Isaf. In an undated project by North for a 'Country House in Snowdonia', Baillie Scott's influence is even more tangible: the main room is labelled 'House Place' and it has a fireplace diagonally in the corner and a curtained dining recess with its own connection to the kitchen. This is exactly what Baillie Scott recommended in *Houses and Gardens* (1906) and indeed carried out at two of his houses, Rose Court and The Crossways.

Voysey's plans were generally less complex and innovative than Baillie Scott's, and his elevations were calmer and more controlled. There is much that links North with Voysey, who, by 1900, had built most of his important houses. 'Simplicity, sincerity, repose, directness and freshness are moral qualities as essential to good architecture as to good men', Voysey stated (1911) – and North would have agreed. Both architects were happy to

exploit the advantages of machine production and modern technology, and both were unrepentant in their use of roughcast irrespective of geographic location. For both men, Gothic was the only true style – that is, a style that, unlike those derived from classicism, had its roots in medieval English society, did not divorce the craftsman from the creative process and could be reinterpreted (by stripping it to the bare minimum) to make functional modern buildings – but this is to jump ahead. For the moment North was enjoying an intensive period of development during which he was establishing the architectural principles that would guide his practice for the rest of his life.

Top. Moorcrag, Windermere (C. F. A. Voysey, 1898-99). The long sweeping roof was typical of North's houses too.
Courtesy of Roger Haigh RIBA

Bottom. 48, Storey's Way, Cambridge (M. H. Baillie Scott, 1912-13).
Courtesy of Patricia McGuire

More of North's sketches of stone cottages, used in his book The Old Cottages of Snowdonia *(Hughes & North 1908). RCAHMW, DI2010_0413*

Domestic Work: 1900–1940

Commissions for private houses provided the staple of North's work throughout his life, accounting for about half of his output (the remainder being church-related). Most of his houses were in north Wales, particularly in or around Llanfairfechan, or in the Conwy valley. The one exception before the First World War was Keldwith in the Lake District, but after the war North won more commissions further afield, such as those in Oxford and Torquay. Apart from Keldwith, none of the domestic commissions were very big; while North might have grasped the opportunity to work on the grand scale more often, he seemed to prefer working at a level that enabled him to manage every aspect himself. He never established a conventional office. In fact, he worked from home, employing assistants only when his prodigious energy alone was insufficient for the task in hand. (His granddaughter remembers office work being abandoned on occasions when the garden or the production of a pageant needed more urgent attention.) The practice of the master delegating the outline design to his assistants to draw up and detail would not have appealed to him.

North was also interested in the small house as a type, with its problems distinct from those of the large country house. In this respect he pursued a course that Baillie Scott had taken in exploring how small houses could be themselves rather than shrunken versions of manor-houses. This interest

A typical stone house, with barn (Cefnbuarddau, Llanaelhaearn).

DI2010_0729, NPRN 26240

No Renaissance Feeling

any Renaissance feeling. The Renaissance, with its foreign pride and pedantry, never took much hold of this part of Wales.

The plan of the dormered cottage is chiefly distinguished from that immediately preceding it by generally having a wooden staircase in the centre of the house, instead of that of stone at one end. This change is owing to the fact that the loft having now developed into three chambers, it was more convenient and private for the stairs to land in the centre room, instead of at one end, making only one passage-room instead of two.

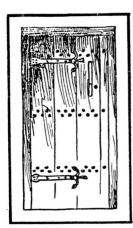

Door to Loft at Tyddyn Pwll.
Probably old front door.

The *fleur de lis* hinges show the remnants of the Gothic tradition continuing down to the eighteenth century.

In the old Vicarage at Clynnog the windows have all been replaced by others of larger size in the early nineteenth century, but at Tyddyn Pwll, a much finer example, in fact possibly the finest, as far as style and proportion is concerned, in our district, two out of three old dormers have their original windows, and one

54

Plas y Person, Clynnog

retains its original glazing. Whether these houses were originally roofed with stone slates, or with thatch, is uncertain. At the main gable-ends we find a thin piece of the wall rising above the slates, as in the earlier buildings like Derwen Deg, where it was doubtless put as a protection to the thatch. This feature, however, does not appear on the

Plas y Person (Old Parsonage), Clynnog.
The windows are not original.

dormers, so it may simply have been a survival, though doubtless, in high gales, it was a protection to the verges of the main gables.

The valleys at the intersection of the dormer with the main roofs are very simply but effectively worked with the slates only, without the use of lead. This method continued till the introduction of large and thin slates rendered it no longer pos-

55

Pages from The Old Cottages of Snowdonia.

(Hughes & North 1908)

led North to the design of mass-housing for the working classes: he entered national competitions for housing schemes in 1918 and 1940; in 1920 he designed a scheme of twenty houses for the Llanfairfechan Urban District Council (not executed), and in 1927 a street of houses in Bangor for the Christian Order in Politics, Economics and Citizenship (COPEC) (see pages 70-1). Another estate in Llanfairfechan (The Close) and a small group of houses in Deganwy form a sort of intermediate category between private houses and mass-housing, like the products of the Garden Village movement in its physical form if not its

administration. The Deganwy houses and The Close were planned estates, but the houses were detached and mostly privately built for specific clients.

From this time it is possible to see North's interest in the distinctive architecture of north-west Wales in his buildings. He took a passionate interest in Welsh history and culture, especially in the old buildings around him, despite the fact that he was an English incomer in Llanfairfechan, where there was a tendency for English-speaking and Welsh-speaking communities to live separate lives. (At Llanfairfechan the Church in Wales held English services in one church and Welsh in the other, and nonconformist chapels were similarly divided on language grounds.) North was one of the first people to appreciate the humble Welsh architectural vernacular as worthy of serious study; he began visiting and measuring cottages and churches, many of them falling into ruin, and it is clear that this interest influenced his own buildings. There were parallels in other fields for this exploration of the vernacular as a source for new work – for instance, Ralph Vaughan Williams (almost exactly North's contemporary) was exploring folk song at the same time.

Local architecture was the subject of his two delightful books, *The Old Churches of Arllechwedd* (1906) and *The Old Cottages of Snowdonia* (1908, with Harold Hughes). There was a romantic side to North's character which, when combined with an antiquarian streak inherited from his father, convinced him that old houses were the survivors of a past that was better attuned to society and the physical environment. There was also the Arts and Crafts upbringing he had absorbed from William Morris and his followers. From them he learned about buildings growing organically from their settings. The very first line in his book about cottages is a quotation from Morris: 'Our teachers must be Nature and History'. Throughout the book he stresses the simplicity of old Welsh houses, their dignity and repose. Later he concludes: 'It is still more important that we should not break into the beautiful harmony of the landscape with something out of tune with the district'. Indeed, so strongly did he believe in this that, while serving on the Llanfairfechan U.D.C. (1904-7), he prepared a report in 1905 recommending visual control over new buildings in the parish. Amongst his suggestions were that second- or third-quality slates should be used in preference to first-quality (because they were thicker); walls should be of stone rather than brick, and if covered with roughcast the colour to be from ochre to white; where brick was used (presumably for chimneys), it should be brindled or red rather than yellow; windows to be in small panes of plain glass; and finally 'creepers are an improvement to any building'.[21] Some of the architectural thinking that North derived from his vernacular studies reflects values that, while in one sense conservative, were, in another, ahead of their time, for example in valuing what we might today call local distinctiveness, appropriateness to the environment and sustainability.

PRIVATE HOUSES

Between the building of Wern Isaf (1900) and the outbreak of the First World War North designed around eighteen houses and cottages. Most of them were modest, and North reused themes from his earlier houses in preference to developing radical new ideas. The geometrical complexities of Wern Isaf he seems to have reserved for himself (apart from Keldwith and the houses at Torquay and Glan Conwy); for the most part the houses had straightforward, orthogonal plans.

The next house to be built after Wern Isaf was Woodcot, Llanfairfechan (1903).

Cefn Isaf, Ro-wen (1904-8): south elevation.

RCAHMW, DS2010_674_003 (top), DS2010_674_007 (bottom), NPRN 472

The open-plan layout used so successfully at his own house was repeated here but much simplified, as the plan was orthogonal, with the reception rooms and hall in a straight line. North placed a pair of doors either side of the central hall, to the dining room one way and to the living room the other. These could divide the ground floor into three separate spaces, or the doors could be folded back to allow all three spaces to flow into one on the long axis. Also in Llanfairfechan, Talfor and Gorsefield (a pair of semi-detached houses, 1906), Whilome (1907), Beamsmoor and Northfield (both 1912) have similar plans. The influence of Baillie

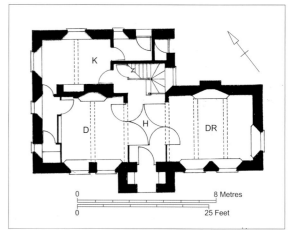

Above. Talfor and Gorsefield, Llanfairfechan (1906).

Adam Voelcker, NPRN 409675

Above right. Plan of Whilome, The Close (1907).

K = Kitchen, D = Dining room, H = Hall, DR = Drawing room

Adam Voelcker, DI2010_0422

Right. Elevation of Whilome.

RCAHMW, DI2009_1393, NPRN 409677

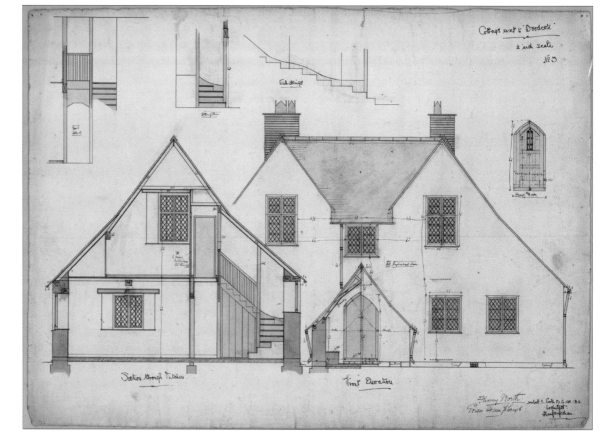

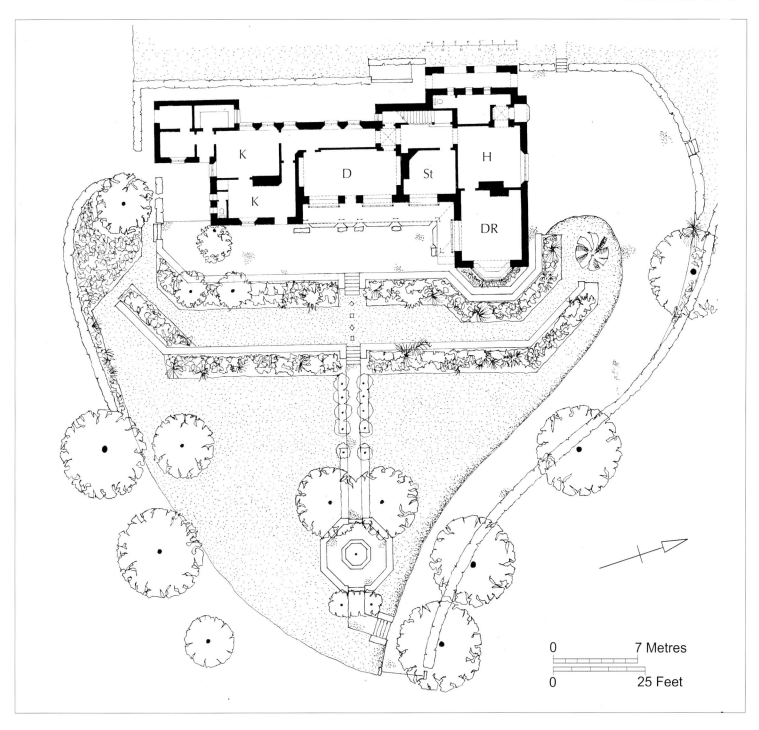

Scott is obvious in the way that wide doors are used to arrange the rooms into one flowing space or a sequence of smaller spaces.

At Cefn Isaf, Ro-wen (1904), North returned to the long single-banked plan of the Hythe house competition, with living rooms facing south and circulation, stairs, bathrooms and other service areas at the rear. The plan is today less clear than the Hythe one, the result of an unanticipated enlargement of the original smallish holiday house to a larger permanent home in 1908. The construction, materials and forms are similar to those at Wern Isaf; so are the lovely details, such as the tiled fireplaces and floors, the front door with

Plan of house and garden, Cefn Isaf, Ro-wen (1904-8).

K = Kitchen, D = Dining room, St = Study, H = Hall, DR = Drawing room

Adam Voelcker, DI2010_0416, NPRN 472

Staircase hall at Cefn Isaf.
RCAHMW, DS2010_674_013,
NPRN 472

Doors at Cefn Isaf.

RCAHMW, DS2010_674_010
(far left), DS2010_674_011 (left),
Adam Voelcker (above),
NPRN 472

its prisms, the window-seats and pierced shutters. If anything has developed beyond Wern Isaf it is the relationship of the house to its garden (also planned by North). At Wern Isaf the two main living rooms look onto the garden through windows with waist-height sills; at Cefn Isaf the windows have become delightful bays opening more fully towards the terraced garden through a veranda, with knee-height sills so as to allow the garden to be seen from a sitting position inside.

Keldwith (1910-11) was the biggest house North ever built. It was planned as a holiday home for Alec Rea, a Liverpool businessman and later High Sheriff of Westmorland. Rea and his American wife had met North while on holiday in north Wales in 1909. The site they chose was in the Lake District, high up above Troutbeck Bridge and looking west towards Windermere.

North's first design proposed an H-plan main house with a service wing, all of two storeys. At the centre was the hall with its inglenook fireplace; at each side were the dining and drawing rooms, facing west towards the magnificent views, their gables projecting beyond the hall to provide shelter for a central veranda. A similar recess at the rear formed the entrance with its porch. The planning was spacious but tightly controlled. There was a certain liveliness to the elevations, the windows responding to views, orientation and room function, but the overall design was somewhat static in failing to engage with the dramatic site.

North or his clients must have recognised this shortcoming, as the design then changed. The basic plan remained, with the living rooms still enjoying the views and the service wing still attached at the north end, but the house grew to three storeys and

Cefn Isaf: drawing room window, looking west.

RCAHMW, DS2010_674_024, NPRN 472

the front (west) projections were splayed out at 45 degrees, in butterfly-plan fashion,[22] giving the house the dynamic and exhilarating quality it had previously lacked. A grand *porte-cochère* was added on the entrance (east) side, with Gothic arches over the carriageway and a cruciform-gabled roof over the first-floor bedroom. The canted front wings also had cruciform roofs and the central part, instead of being lower and contained between the side wings, rose up to the full height of the house and had a gable of its own. The drama of the site seems to have been embraced in this final design.

There was a dramatic quality to the interior of Keldwith too (until the house was subdivided into three in the 1950s). Arriving at the house through the *porte-cochère* one entered a large vestibule which offered access to the cloaks, the drawing

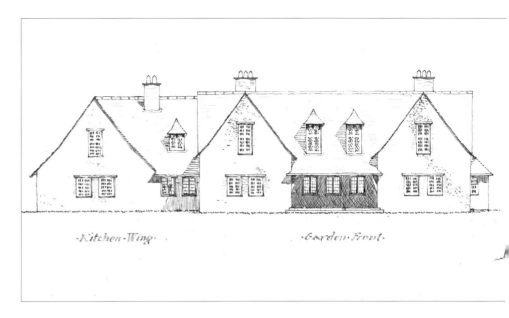

Keldwith, Windermere (1910-11): early scheme.
RCAHMW, DI2008_1269

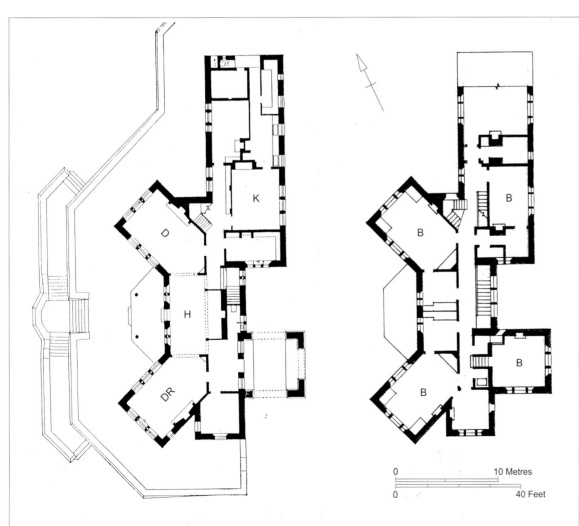

Keldwith: west elevation, from north-west.
Adam Voelcker

Floor plans, as built.
D = Dining room, H = Hall,
DR = Drawing room,
K = Kitchen, B = Bedroom
Adam Voelcker, DI2010_0419

Keldwith: west elevation, from north-west.

RCAHMW, DS2009_198_003

Below. Entrance elevation (porte-cochère on right, later gazebo on left).

RCAHMW, DS2009_198_001

room or the hall. To go further into the house one had to go through the hall and past the big inglenook fireplace which, inserted in the circulation spine, broke what would have otherwise been a very long passage. More drama was provided by the relationship of the hall to the dining and drawing rooms, which interconnected around the two 45-degree corners, as at Wern Isaf.

The house was built of the local stone, tightly laid with the locally characteristic unmortared joints and without North's usual roughcast. The working drawings show bands of slate between the stone rubble but in the event these were omitted. The roofs are of green Westmorland slate and the

Left. Keldwith: bedroom.
RCAHMW, DS2009_198_016

Below. Keldwith: hall with inglenook.
RCAHMW, DS2009_198_009

chimneys of stone. The windows have timber casements, some with small panes, projecting slate hoods and sills, and grey limestone mullions duplicated inside with hexagonal oak posts. All external openings are rectangular or square; the only non-rectangular heads are the *porte-cochère* arches (similar to those used at the Talycafn gatehouse) and the external doorway of the hall, where pointed arches are used symbolically to celebrate the threshold between inside and outside.

The internal detailing was carefully considered and beautifully crafted (and much of it survives despite the conversion). The main living rooms are lined with wide sheets of dark, varnished elm with slender cover-strips hiding the joints. The panelling extends up to a continuous shelf about one foot below ceiling level, its edge delicately scalloped in the way that E. S. Prior liked. Above the shelf the remaining wall and the ceiling are painted white, the joists and beams rough-sawn and contrasting with the finer joinery below. The design of the doors follows a rigorous hierarchy of detail, from the wide front door, the most intricate, to the bedroom cupboard doors, the plainest; all have delightful fittings in the best Arts and Crafts tradition. The fireplaces have surrounds of De Morgan tile and mantel-shelves supported on carved shafts of green slate.

An illustrated description of Keldwith was published in *Small Country Houses of Today* (Weaver 1922: 46-51). The author Lawrence Weaver was enthusiastic about the house as a 'refreshing revival of Gothic principles'. He admired the way North could work in a 'medieval manner' despite the stylistic tendencies of the majority of other architects, yet at the same time incorporate 'modern equipment' (such as basins in bedroom cupboards and secondary glazing). 'I could not help feeling that John Ruskin would have felt justified in Mr North as one of his children,' he continued. He also liked North's 'ingenious handling of the sun-trap plan'. It is indeed well done and one feels that North was in his element playing with the diagonal geometry he first used at Wern Isaf.

Keldwith marks the highpoint of North's career as a domestic architect, and the house ranks high amongst the very good Arts and Crafts houses that line the shores of Windermere, not least Voysey's Broadleys, built just a few years earlier. The confidence with which the house is handled – the response to the site, the massing of the external

forms and the integrity of the detailing – demonstrates that North was more than competent as a country house architect. Yet, his inclination was always towards houses which were not grand or formal, and Keldwith's expansive character was probably a response to his clients' requirements. When North entered the 1912 *Country Life* Competition for a Holiday Cottage and Garden there was another opportunity to design something rather imposing (the house was to have eight rooms at a cost of £550, a motor-house for £100 and a garden for £150). The winning entries were indeed grand and formal, the houses being symmetrical and tending towards classical style, but North's scheme shied away from formality, its style being relaxed and picturesque. Lawrence Weaver, who assessed the competition with Lutyens and Arthur Bolton, was guarded in his praise of North's house, calling it 'an individual conception' (Weaver 1913: 131).

After 1918 North continued building small houses, most of them in north Wales but a few further afield: he designed a butterfly-plan house in Torquay (1925, now much altered), a house and consulting room for a Dr Guthrie in Higher Bebington, Wirral (1931) and he returned to the butterfly-plan

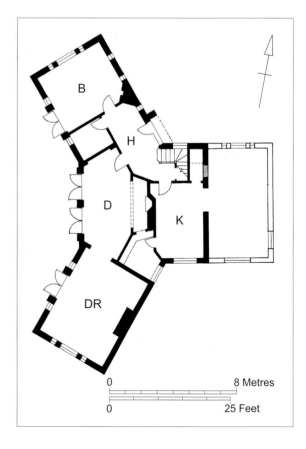

Hafod, Glan Conwy (1935): ground floor plan. Extended eastwards later.

B = Bedroom, H = Hall, D = Dining room, K = Kitchen, DR = Drawing room

Adam Voelcker

at Hafod, Glan Conwy (1935, originally Arsyllfa). It is at The Close in Llanfairfechan, however, which he developed as an estate on his own land from 1923 to 1940, that we see the best examples of his post-war domestic work. 'The houses, which are of picturesque design and sound construction, with town water, main drainage and gas, are labour saving in plan and fittings, and each one is built to suit the requirements of the Purchaser at very reasonable cost,' stated his advertisement (*see* page 126). A lane ran uphill from the Church Institute on Park Road, turned round a small brow and then meandered along the hillside before returning to Park Road. Some of the houses were built in contemporaneous groups, some singly. Towards the bottom of the estate the houses looked to each other across the lane; further up they took advantage of the view towards Anglesey. The house designs followed a fairly limited set of forms, internal layouts and details, and North's interest extended outside the house to the design of tiny detached garages, outhouses and even the garden boundaries of

Hafod: west elevation.
Adam Voelcker

Key to Llanfairfechan

A   Plas Llanfair Cottage
B   Northcot
C   Church Institute
D   Churchmen's Club
E   1-4 Bryn Haul
F   Beamsmoor
G   Wern Isaf

ST WINIFRED'S SCHOOL

H   Plas Llanfair
I   Chapel
J   Ida North music wing
K   Hall
L   Classroom wing
M   Sanatorium

THE CLOSE

1   Northfield
2   Brooklands
3   Coedfa
4   The Haven
5   Bolnhurst
6   Tŷ'n Coed (Woodcot)
7   Whilome
8   Rose Lea
9   Tŷ Hwnt yr Afon
10   Hillcroft (Llys Hywel)
11   Maes Aled (Cloud End)
12   Parciau (Westernie)
13   Araulfan
14   Trewen
15   Efrydfa
16   Carreg Fran (Crowstones)
17   Bryn Ffawydd
18   Ael-y-gwynt
19   Acorn Cottage
20   Carreg Lwyd
(post-1940 house by Padmore)
21   Hillcrest
22   Grey Gables
23   Dwyfor
24   Greenhills
25   Neuadd Wen

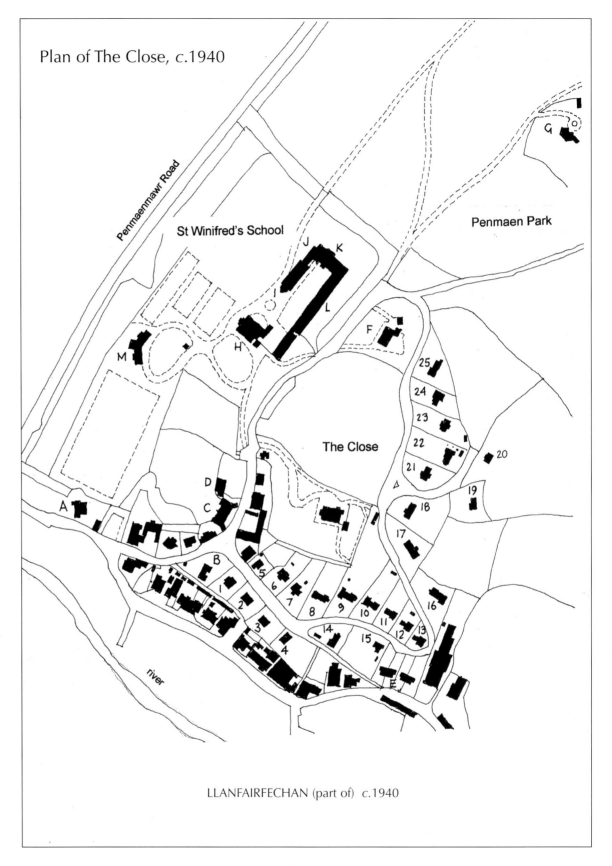

Plan of The Close, c.1940

LLANFAIRFECHAN (part of) c.1940

vertical slates wired together to make a fence in the traditional way. Wern Isaf lay in fields beyond the estate to the north-east. North planned an extension to the estate but the outbreak of the Second World War prevented its implementation.

Some of the houses in The Close were built speculatively (or at least started thus), others were for specific clients, usually local professionals – people such as solicitors, teachers (some from St Winifred's School) and local businessmen. Many of these people were probably already known to North, but he did not socialise easily and Padmore recalls that he never made close friends of his clients, and preferred to avoid women clients as they interfered too much.[23]

The Close has similarities with some of the Garden Village estates built in the pre-war and inter-war periods elsewhere in Wales, for instance at Rhiwbina, north Cardiff.[24] However, the similarity is on an aesthetic rather than social level.

Aerial views of The Close, Llanfairfechan, showing (left) houses nos. 9-13 and (below) nos. 18-25.

RCAHMW, AP_2010_2249 (left), AP_2010_2245 (below)

The Close, Llanfairfechan.

Adam Voelcker

The Garden Village movement originated in the need to provide housing for worker-tenants. This included not only the provision of healthy houses but also gardens for growing vegetables and shared open spaces to help engender a feeling of community amongst the estates' inhabitants. By contrast, The Close was built incrementally over a few decades and in a more relaxed manner than the more formal Garden Village estates; its inhabitants were owner-occupiers from the middle classes, and there was no provision of communal space. North's intentions were not altruistic. He owned land – the seeds of developing it began with the pre-war houses at the bottom of the hill and then flourished as he sold off more and more plots. He loved designing new houses – each plot

Dwyfor, The Close (1937).
RCAHMW, DS2010_669_001,
NPRN 411860

55

brought the potential of a fresh design and North could be in (almost) total control of the appearance of each and ultimately of 'his' entire garden village.

If he had a social vision in mind it was revealed in his planning of the nearby St Winifred's School rather than at The Close (see Chapter 5).

North designed two other estates of detached, individual houses. One was for a new village at Llanddulas, east of Colwyn Bay, for R. O. F. Wynne of Garthewin. Nothing is known about this unbuilt scheme, but North did design three houses in Minffordd Road, Llanddulas in 1937.[25] The other scheme was built in 1933 at Vardre Park, Deganwy. Unlike The Close, it was not built on family land but for a developer, R. Arthur Jones, who originally planned a bigger estate. Only five houses were built, arrayed in echelon formation beside the main road to West Shore. They are perky little objects, with high hipped roofs, stepped chimneys and rather exaggerated features. They are less relaxed than the houses in The Close, perhaps because the layout is more regimented, and, though picturesque with their multi-coloured slates, they are not amongst the best of North's domestic work.

Opposite page. Ael-y-gwynt, The Close (1936).
RCAHMW, DS2007_404_003 (top), DS2007_404_002 Bottom), NPRN 406860

Left. Trewen, The Close (1931).
RCAHMW, DS2007_403_001, NPRN 406859

Below. Rhiwbina Garden Village, Cardiff (by Raymond Unwin and A. M. Mottram, 1912-1923).
RCAHMW, DS2008_187_006, NPRN 403393

THE DETAILED DESIGN OF NORTH'S HOUSES

Right. Vardre Park, Deganwy (1933).

RCAHMW, DS2010_657_001, NPRN 409685

Below right. Brooklands, The Close (1922).

Adam Voelcker, NPRN 409681

Below. 'We are Seven' memorial, Conwy parish church.

Adam Voelcker

The steep roughcast gable became perhaps North's most recognisable trademark (and not just in The Close houses). His love of characterful roofs and good roof materials and detailing was expressed in all his buildings, with the gables a key part of the overall design. North did not have one preferred roof angle as Lutyens reputedly did but was more pragmatic, generally choosing an angle between 52 and 55.5 degrees from the horizontal (though often steeper for churches). His gables usually start steeply at the top, then broaden out to about 45 degrees further down. (Even his little 'We are Seven' memorial in Conwy churchyard, made out of a lattice of metal steel flats, has a cross-section of this shape, so it must have been dear to North.) The roofs often swoop down to head height, giving ample storage space in the eaves. Unlike Voysey, who preferred horizontality of form as it provided a sense of repose, North (who was known by his colleagues as 'long-roof North' [26]), loved steepness and verticality – he even used artistic licence to steepen roof angles in his sketches for *The Old Cottages of Snowdonia*.

The architectural writer, Phil Thomas, sees these pointed gables as a metaphor for the mountains of Snowdonia.[27] More prosaically, they shed the Welsh rain well and the verticality allows lofty bedrooms with tall windows, another common feature of many of North's houses. Frequently the gables are paired closely, so that the valley between them is higher than the eaves to either side. Where there was a projecting porch below the gables, the valley down-pipe drained onto the porch roof; but where the porch was recessed there was no neat way to carry the down-pipe to ground level, and North resorted to running a pipe from the valley to one or other of the eaves gutters. It is an ungainly arrangement, but one seen repeatedly; one concludes that North justified it on functional grounds. Eaves

gutters discharged via canted down-pipes rather than swan-neck bends – perhaps for stylistic reasons, or because they could be cleared more easily.

North's roofs were usually of Welsh slate, preferably laid to diminishing courses using thick random-width slates from unmechanised quarries around Snowdon.[28] 'Nothing can atone for a roof of hard thin slates of even texture and colour', he argued in his book on Snowdonian cottages (Hughes & North 1908: 72). Sometimes the slates were uniform in colour, sometimes multi-coloured and sometimes incorporating lozenge patterns of contrasting purple and green. Timber barge-boards were generally avoided: North tended to prefer the simpler, traditional detail of plain, slated verges. Dormers appeared in a variety of sizes and shapes (gabled, hipped, catslide), all of them seen commonly in vernacular buildings and described

Above. Typical canted rainwater pipe (Ael-y-gwynt, The Close).
RCAHMW, DS2010_671_008, NPRN 406860

Right. Conical fléche, Church Institute, Llanfairfechan.
RCAHMW, DS2010_ 658_006, NPRN 471

Dormers: Parciau, The Close (above), Church Institute (above, right).

RCAHMW, DS2010_661_009, DS2010_658_007, NPRN 409750 & 471

in his book, but if bedrooms could be lit through a gable window this was preferable.

North enjoyed designing chimneys, which often become tiny gabled buildings in themselves (a good example is the central chimney to the octagonal lodge at Newry (now Plas Heulog), where a cruciform cluster of four gabled brick shafts supports a fifth, set diagonally). He, like Philip Webb, always made a point of ensuring his fireplaces would draw satisfactorily.

Chimneys: Vardre Park, Deganwy (above), Ael-y-gwynt, The Close (right).

RCAHMW, DS2010_657_002, DS2010_671_012, NPRN 409685 & 406860

The walls were built of two-foot thick rubble stone before the First World War and brickwork after, using a 'rat-trap' bond which allowed a partial cavity, thus controlling damp ingress and also economising in material.[29] North's preferred wall-finish of roughcast (or wet-dash) has already been mentioned, and he tended to use it on most of his buildings, whether the walls were built of stone or of brick. Since the stonework of his very first buildings was not covered, it is interesting to speculate why he later chose to use roughcast – did the stonework let in the rain or did he like the appearance? Comments in his book suggest that both reasons played a part. No specifications for the mortar mix survive, but it will have consisted of local aggregates mixed together with lime (and probably cement too, as its use became more prevalent), thrown onto the wall and then painted white.

Chimneys: lodge, Newry, Llanfairfechan (above), Dwyfor, The Close (left).

RCAHMW, DS2010_666_003, DS2010_669_005, NPRN 86454 & 411860

Above. Beamsmoor, Llanfairfechan (1912). Note the similarity to the early scheme for Keldwith (page 47).

RCAHMW, DS2010_672_004, NPRN 470

Right. Gothic arch porch and front door (Ael-y-gwynt).

RCAHMW, DS2010_671_004, DS2010_671_009, NPRN 406860

Windows were usually small-paned cottage-casement type. Only once (at Northcot) did he use vertical sliding sash windows, and he reluctantly specified the leaded glazing favoured by many Arts and Crafts architects (usually only if the client insisted, as at Whilome and Grey Gables). Windows were often square or rectangular at ground level, taller and narrower at upper level, to fit more comfortably into the high gables and perhaps to provide better ventilation. Semicircular window heads were used at some of the earlier houses (such as Bolnhurst), cambered heads occasionally (at Woodcot and Cefn Isaf), but straightforward rectangular or square shapes were his preferred option. North's favoured material was metal, copying the timber ones he used before the war. The windows were produced by Henry Hope & Sons and chosen from a range of cottage-style versions whose standard proportions North was able to change to suit his own aesthetic preferences. He even had a hand in producing Hope's catalogue.[30] It is perhaps surprising that a devoted Morris disciple should specify factory-produced components, but North was not alone in accepting the inevitability of mass-production if economy was to be achieved.

Porch entrances and front doorways were given special, even symbolic, treatment. Whereas Voysey's were often semicircular, North's usually had pointed arches, the porch with a sweeping Gothic arch descending nearly to ground level, the front door with a shallow-arched, almost triangular, head. Front doors tended to be quite wide, often made of a single piece of hardwood on the outside and criss-crossed with bracing inside like medieval doors or gates. Sometimes (as at Wern Isaf and Cefn Isaf) they were decorated with tiny prisms of glass acting as spyholes.

Internal detailing, like the external forms, tended to be from a limited range, repeated from house to house. The character of these details in general was simple and 'serviceable'. As North pointed out in his book, 'The interior of these old houses is entirely dependent for its effect upon the simplest means: that of just showing the construction, instead of concealing it, as in most modern work.' (Hughes & North 1908: 63) North liked to see ceiling joists and beams exposed as in traditional Welsh cottages; he did not conceal them or 'distress' them to look old, but sometimes painted

Front door at Cefn Isaf, Ro-wen.
Adam Voelcker, NPRN 472

Exposed ceiling beams, typical of a sixteenth-century Snowdonian house (Pant Glas Uchaf).
RCAHMW, DI2010_0737

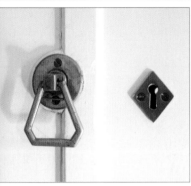

Above. Wooden and brass door furniture.

Adam Voelcker

(Below) RCAHMW, DS2010_674_032

them with stencilled patterns. The timber was usually rough-sawn, not planed, even when finer, joinery-quality work such as panelling was fitted below. Keldwith is an early example; it also occurs at Whitefriars, Llanfairfechan as late as 1933.

Interior doors in the pre-War houses were usually boarded vertically and braced horizontally, with wooden latches and finger holes; after the War North usually specified imported panelled doors, with five or six horizontal panels. Partitions were

Right. Built-in cupboards and drawers, Cefn Isaf, Ro-wen.

RCAHMW, DS2010_674_029 (top), DS2010_674_030 (below), NPRN 472

Landing at Wern Isaf, Llanfairfechan.
RCAHMW, DS2010_076_036, NPRN 17037

often boarded rather than plastered, with thin cover-strips over the vertical joints rather than tongue and groove (cupboard doors were treated in the same way). This was perhaps North's modern version of the traditional oak boarded partition, which he described at length in his book. Simple, brass window and door furniture was chosen from catalogues.[31]

Staircases and balustrades were utilitarian and frankly plain when compared even with those by lesser architects working in north Wales, who often used elegant tapered newels surmounted with wide cappings in the style of Voysey. Spatially, North's staircases were always successful, often turning through 90 degrees so that space was enclosed or a corner defined. Most of his staircases incorporated winders to save space. Where floors were not timber-boarded, they were usually paved in red quarry tiles, with olive-green and white insets in a variety of patterns depending on the importance of the room.

North devoted much care to window openings: in thick stone walls the reveals splayed back each side at 45 degrees to let in the daylight, a traditional and attractive feature which, to North's regret, was not possible in thinner, brick walls. Some windows had internal shutters (at Wern Isaf each set has a different pattern of perforation) and those in the living rooms often had seats set into the window recess.

Window seat at Cefn Isaf, Ro-wen and above, window shutters at Wern Isaf.
RCAHMW, DS2010_674_023, DS2010_076_031, NPRN 472

Above. Tiled fireplace at Wern Isaf and above right, Northcot and right, brick fireplace at Tan-y-coed, Llanfair Talhaearn.

RCAHMW, DS2010_076_034 (above),
Adam Voelcker (above right),
Adam Voelcker (right),
NPRN 17037, 409680 & 409744

The design of the fireplace, the symbolic hearth, was always important to North, both in appearance and in functionality. Many were made of brown, brindled bricks from Hancocks of Buckley. Some had Gothic-arched openings with tiled surrounds and sometimes, as at Wern Isaf, elaborate mantels and shelving. Setting the fireplace within an ingle was a favourite device of many Arts and Crafts architects, including North. His book features delightful sketches of traditional fireplaces. Fine examples of the way he put this inspiration into practice can be seen at Bolnhurst, Beamsmoor, Keldwith and also at the Churchmen's Club and the Church Institute, Llanfairfechan.

PUBLIC HOUSING

For someone who enjoyed economy for its own sake and was perhaps happiest at the small scale, it was not a large leap from the design of cottages to the layout of public housing. North kept abreast by reading architectural journals, and his scrapbooks are filled, particularly in the 1930s, with photographs and articles of small architect-designed houses, which must have appealed to his sense of what was economical and utilitarian but also good-looking. Had he been working on the continent a little earlier (and been sympathetic to the Functionalist aesthetic), one can imagine him taking delight in the challenge of designing German Existenzminimum flats. Frank Tyldesley, who built many of North's houses, recalled that North had a reputation for building houses cheaper than other builders, not through skimping but by being constantly vigilant of cost. North was economical with his room planning, too, using every space to full advantage and, where awkward corners resulted, using them for cupboards.

North's first involvement with public housing came towards the end of the First World War when he entered a national competition in 1918 for the design of working-class cottages. It was organised by the Local Government Board (LGB) through the Royal Institute of British Architects (RIBA) in anticipation of the necessary post-war expansion of public housing and was divided into six regional sectors. North entered for the Manchester and Liverpool areas (which included Lancashire, Westmorland, Derbyshire and the northern half of Wales) and prepared his freehand drawings in northern France where he was on active service with the Red Cross. (His scrapbooks at this date were filled with photos of churches in the Haute-Marne region. He also spent his spare time designing a bed-frame for supporting soldiers' broken limbs.)

The competition set four categories of house. Class A was for a living room, scullery and three bedrooms; Class B for the same plus a parlour; Class C for the same but with two bedrooms; and Class D was a variation of A, B or C but with the

Entry for LGB/RIBA housing competition (1918).

RIBA Library Drawings Collection

IV. MANCHESTER AND LIVERPOOL AREA : CLASS A, FIRST PREMIUM.

H. L. North (Llanfairfechan).

bedrooms mainly on the ground floor. A total of 365 entries was received for the Manchester and Liverpool areas alone. They were assessed by a panel of architects, a cleric, a builder and 'two wives of two classes of working men'. The results and some of the designs were reported in two of the national building journals (The Builder 1918; The Building News 1918). Entrants were expected to give due consideration to economical planning, simplicity, the avoidance of unnecessary ornament, and suitability for mass-production and new methods of construction, but they did not need to comply with current by-laws. At the practical level good cross-ventilation was encouraged, as was undercover access to coal stores, and it was noted that 'materials of the locality, if reasonably obtainable, should be specified'. It was not essential that a bathroom be provided, but the w.c. should not be placed in a bathroom or entered from the scullery.

On the whole the assessors seem to have been disappointed by the quality of the schemes and the failure of many to answer adequately the basic requirements. This is hardly surprising given the retrogressive nature of the brief. As Mark Swenarton pointed out in Homes Fit for Heroes (1981), the LGB were not looking for an improvement in housing standards. Indeed, they believed improvement impossible if strict economy was to be achieved in the straitened circumstances of the time. Thus, the type of house called for in the competition was little better than the pre-War council house. This approach was in direct contrast to that of the Tudor Walters committee, appointed in 1917 to investigate the technicalities of the housing programme.[32] Largely through its main member, Raymond Unwin, it argued that economy was possible only if major improvements in housing standards were made.

Within the flawed requirements of the competition brief North did well. The conservative orthodoxy of the LGB and the brief probably suited him. He won first prize in Class A and second in Classes C and D. In Class A he was 'the only competitor who [has] mastered the old-world traditional cottage manner suitable for the countryside', with elevations 'in every way scholarly and admirable' (The Building News, 20th February 1918: 140-2). His scheme proposed a terrace of six cottages: the middle two had wide frontages and were set back on the front elevation

Portrait of North in army uniform during the First World War.

Courtesy of Pamela J. Phillips, DI2009_1386

from the outer pair at each end, which were of deeper, narrower plan with hipped roofs.[33] The walls were of roughcast brick and the roofs of small rough slates cut from quarry waste. On the front elevation the eaves swooped up and down over the bedroom windows, a quaint feature which seems not to have convinced all the assessors. Criticisms included the narrowness of his doors and staircases, and his over-generous larders. His plans were generally approved, however, and his arrangement of larder, scullery and coal-store was deemed 'excellent and well-considered'. His entries for Class C and D were similar to each other and, instead of the wavy eaves, he chose to bring the roof down to the level of the ground-floor door-head, with the bedrooms lit by catslide dormer

windows and a tall, steep gable accentuating the second and fifth cottage in the row of six – more recognisably garden village in style.

In 1920 North designed a scheme of housing for Llanfairfechan Urban District Council. The houses were to be semi-detached, with the entrance, staircase, bathroom and scullery in a strip on the north side, and the living room and parlour on the south. No constructional details are shown on North's surviving drawing, but the walls were probably to be of roughcast brick and the roofs of slate. The style was familiar – a pair of steep gables neatly containing a recessed portion at the centre. It was all straightforward and sensible. The only indulgence was the Gothic arch to the fireplace. The scheme was not built (nor do North's

Proposed housing for Llanfairfechan UDC (1920). RCAHMW, DI2010_1115

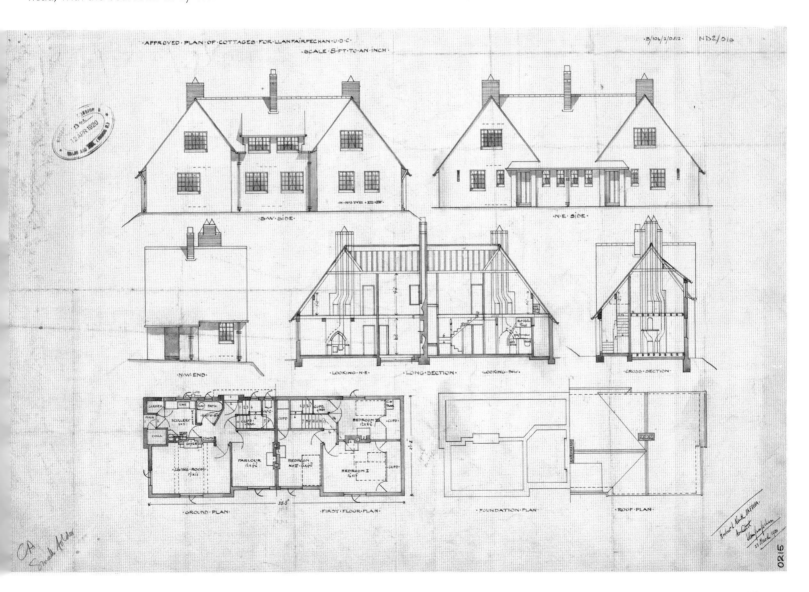

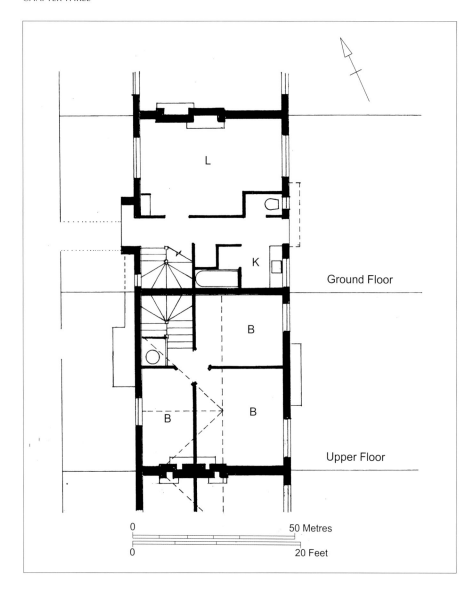

L

K

Ground Floor

B

B

B

Upper Floor

0   50 Metres

0   20 Feet

COPEC housing at Seiriol Road, Bangor (1927).

L = Living room, K = Kitchen, B = Bedroom

Adam Voelcker, DI2010_0417 (above), DS2010_656_003 (right), NPRN 409745

competition entries appear to have led to any housing commissions), but two pairs of semi-detached houses, with similar elevations but different plans to those of the scheme, were erected in 1925 (Nos 1-4 Bryn Haul, Llanfairfechan).

In 1927 North was involved in a housing project that did get built. His client was the Bangor COPEC Housing Group, a branch of the Christian Order in Politics, Economics and Citizenship, which campaigned for a nationwide improvement in housing standards. A regional conference was held in Bangor in 1924, a survey was carried out in 1926 and a year later twenty houses were built, for £8,000, in Seiriol Road, Bangor. The layout consists of two long terraces facing each other across the street. The house plans are mirrored as semi-detached pairs, and North exploited his favourite twin-gable motif to reduce the monotony of the repeated units. The eaves to the street elevation come down quite low, then extend over the projecting porches. A little window tucked below the eaves lights the staircase as it follows the roof up to the three bedrooms. On the ground floor the

big living room spans the full depth of the house and so faces both the street and the garden. Circulation from front door to back door is not through the living room but through the front hall and the scullery. The internal bathroom is between the dog-leg stair and the scullery, and the w.c. is next to the back door, off the scullery. The houses were built of roughcast cavity brick walls on a concrete raft, with a slate roof.

At the time, these houses were regarded locally as setting a benchmark for good-quality social housing, certainly far superior to the slums which they replaced, and unmatched by the sort of housing being built by Bangor City Council, which tended to favour the comfortless and draughty through-living-room. North's plan showed that

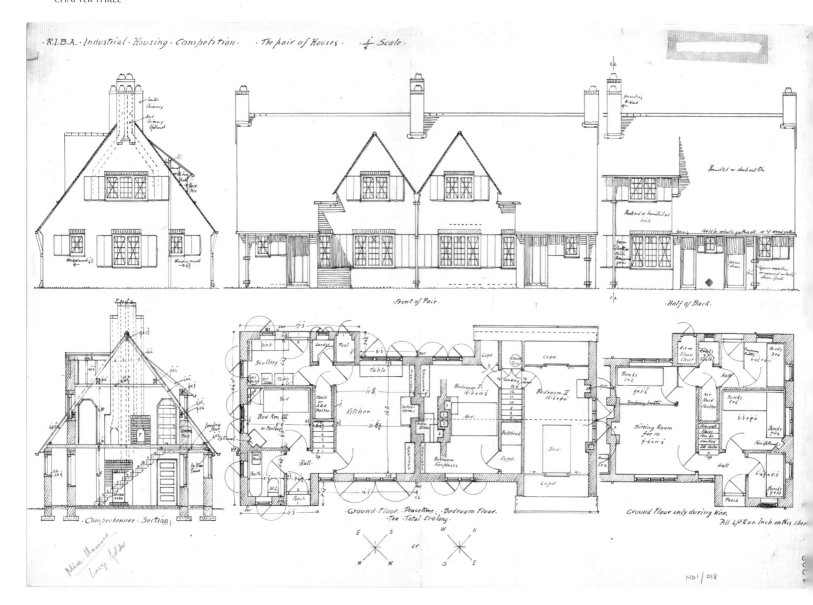

Entry for RIBA Industrial Housing Competition (1940). RCAHMW, DI2008_1264

separating living space from circulation routes was a real improvement, and it is perhaps not entirely coincidental that, after 1929, the council adopted North's arrangement. In fact, it went a step or two further by providing porches at front and back (because of the Bangor rain and wind) and putting the bathrooms upstairs.

North's final public housing designs may have been the last scheme he ever worked on, completed just six months before he died. In July 1940 the Royal Institute of British Architects launched a competition for the design of 'industrial housing', that is, houses that were cheap and simple to build, and could suit conditions both during the Second

World War (such as bomb protection and blackout) and be adapted to future peacetime use. Competitors were asked to propose designs for an estate of 250 such houses at a density of 8 to 12 per acre. Economy of layout and upkeep was essential, as was camouflage from the air, 160 entries were sent in, amongst them schemes by Frederick Gibberd and Ernö Goldfinger.[34] North prepared a drawing of the cross-section and elevations of a two-storey house and the plans illustrating wartime and peacetime layouts, but it is not clear if he did drawings of the estate – nor even if he submitted his entry, which, it has to be said, was not well resolved. Entrants were urged to give careful thought to blast and

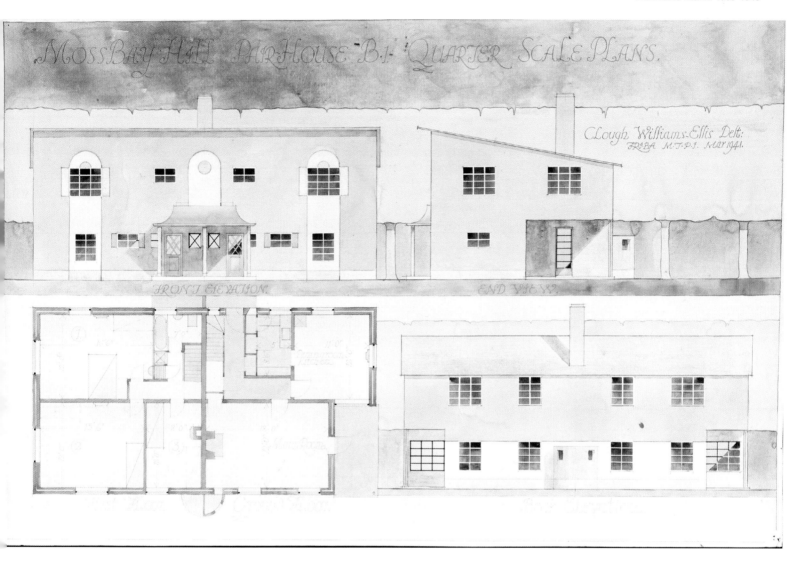

MossBay Hall PairHouse B.1 Quarter Scale Plans.

Clough Williams-Ellis Delt: FRIBA M.T.P.I. MAY 1941.

FRONT ELEVATION   *END VIEW.*

splinter protection, particularly for the bedrooms, which had to be in effect air-raid shelters. Many of the entrants suggested the temporary bricking-up of the bedroom windows (with vents provided), but North simply proposed wooden shutters ('painted Brunswick Green') and a tiny air-raid shelter in the slot for the future (peace-time) staircase. Although he showed alternative plans for the single-storey wartime house and the two-storey peacetime one, he drew elevations only for the latter, showing the happier, prettier peacetime version, with his usual steep gables, cottage-casement windows and busy chimneys. An interesting comparison can be made with a scheme prepared around the same time by Clough Williams-Ellis. It was not for the same competition but for workers' housing at Workington in Cumberland, and Clough positively delighted in horizontal Crittall windows, flat-topped chimneys and shallow mono-pitched concrete roofs (Haslam 1996: 84-5).

Workers' housing at Workington, Cumberland (Clough Williams-Ellis, 1941).

RIBA Library Drawings Collection. Courtesy of the Trustees of the Clough Williams-Ellis Foundation

CHAPTER FOUR

Church Work

Though domestic work occupied a large part of North's professional life, it was the church work that fired his passion most, for through it he could express both his love of architecture and his deep religious belief. In his obituary in the RIBA Journal (May 1941) P. M. Padmore wrote 'Throughout his career he was never happier than when designing churches, or restoring and redecorating them'.

Apart from unexecuted designs for a few new churches, all of North's early church work was for fittings and decoration at existing ones.[35] An important influence on this work was *The Parson's Handbook*, written in 1899 by the Revd Percy Dearmer. It was an attempt to return the Church to the native English form of liturgy with its emphasis on beautiful and dignified ceremonial. Dearmer encouraged art and music in churches, stressing that 'Nothing should be put into the church that is not the best of its kind.'(Dearmer 1921: 79). While a curate in Lambeth in 1891 Dearmer had introduced Morris coverings for the altar – it was always Morris textiles that North used later in his own church work. Dearmer gave sound practical advice on the design of church interiors and fittings right from the start of his book (which continued to be published and revised until 1932) – about the relationship of nave to chancel ('A church is not a theatre'), about lighting (both natural and artificial), about the detailed design of fixtures and furniture. He even gave a recipe for distemper, encouraging the use of plain walls as a contrast to the richly decorated altar and reredos. He recommended incumbents to seek proper advice on all these aspects, mentioning the Church Crafts League which he had helped to establish in 1890 for that very purpose. The organisation had representatives throughout Britain, and North was their man in Wales. Through the League North obtained a

number of church jobs of his own and probably advised on many others.

One of North's very first church jobs was at Saints Andrew and Bartholomew at Ashleworth in Gloucestershire, where he designed the new reredos and altar furniture in 1899.[36] Jobs that came to him through the League were furnishings at Cwm Penmachno, Conwy (1907), and furnishings and decorative work at Cellan, Ceredigion (1908-9). The work at Cellan also involved some rebuilding of this small country church. The north wall of the chancel and the east wall of the porch were rebuilt, and the windows were remodelled in a modern Gothic idiom using brick jambs and centre piers and (typical of North) arch-heads that hardly curved. He designed a very simple open rood screen to fit in front of the chancel arch and built a new ceiling in the chancel, ready for his painted decoration. Much as North admired Morris, and

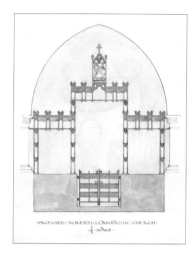

Design for screen at St Madoc, Llanbadoc Fawr (Gwent).

RCAHMW, DI2010_0404, NPRN 96655

All Saints, Cellan, near Lampeter: ceiling decoration (1908).

Adam Voelcker, NPRN 404146

Church of the Holy Spirit, Harlescott, Shrewsbury (1934-36): east elevation (early photograph).

RCAHMW, DI2010_0398

75

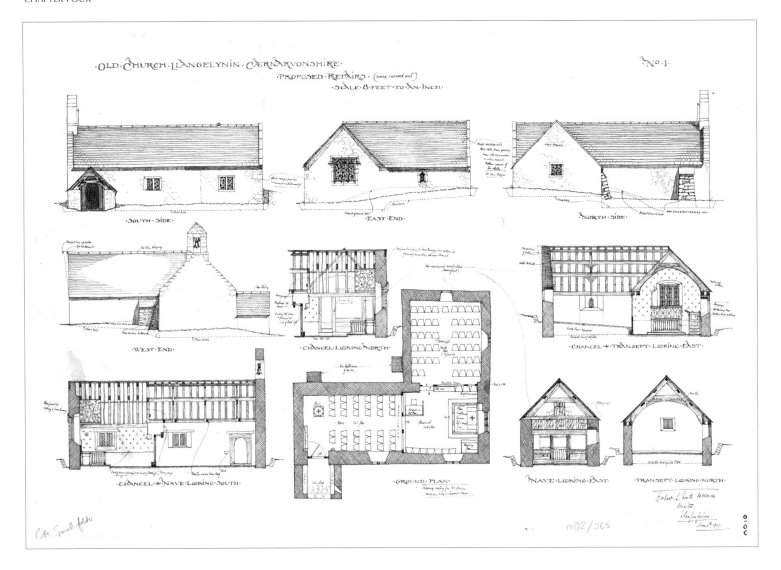

Proposed repairs at St Celynin, Llangelynin, Conwy (1907).

RCAHMW, DI2010_0414, NRPRN 43864

also the timeless quality of old unspoilt churches, he seems not to have been a gentle church restorer of the sort encouraged by Morris and the SPAB. He was keen on putting his own mark on old buildings, unlike his less imaginative colleague Harold Hughes, who sensitively repaired many of the older churches in the diocese but designed only one new church.[37]

In 1909 North reinstated the loft to the fine medieval screen at St Mary and All Saints, Conwy, not by providing an imitation of the former parapet in oak but by simply putting a Morris hanging in its place. In 1910 he designed the fittings, decoration and reordering at Christ Church, Stafford (now demolished) and in 1913 decoration and furnishings at Butterfield's St Mary, Aberystwyth. After the First World War he designed fittings for the two churches at Llanfairfechan: at Christ Church in 1921 and at

St Mary's in 1925.[38] There was little of the sumptuous or gorgeous in North's fittings and he did not use extravagantly rich materials (nor did he fabricate the work himself, unlike Wilson and others). He used wood and iron mostly, carving them simply and painting them in pretty blues and greens often set off by the sparing use of stronger colours or gilding. His altars were dignified with dossals and wings in the 'English altar' tradition continued by Ninian Comper, often using Morris & Co fabrics for the curtains and coverings. His decorative schemes, mostly applied to ceilings and roof timbers, were characterised by sparse stencil-like patterns of meandering vegetation, always delicate and controlled, never garish, and, as Ian Allan points out, 'graphic work rather than painting' in technique (Allan 1988: 176). His wife

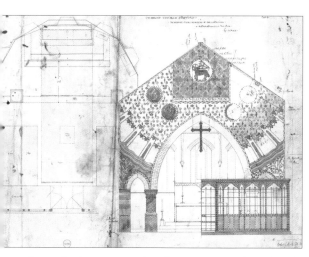

Design for decorative work and new screen at Christ Church, Stafford (1910).

RCAHMW, DI2008_1359

Screen at St Mary, Llanfairfechan (1925).

Adam Voelcker, NPRN 301809

Ida may have carried out some of this decorative work. A letter to the incumbent of Capel Curig church is typical of his modest approach: '...you really only require a small sum to produce a very great transformation to your church ... in fact, if you spent more the result would not be at all better there is such a thing as overdoing things, is there not?'[39]

Though North enjoyed designing church fittings, he perhaps got more satisfaction, given his creative

Design for reredos at Caerhun church (1904). The church was never built.

RCAHMW, DI2008_0152

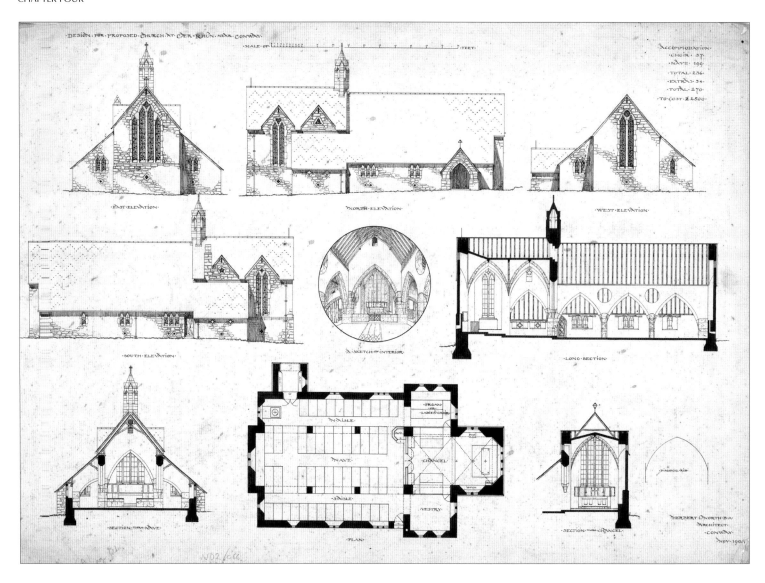

Design for a proposed church at Caerhun (1902).

RCAHMW, DI2010_0415

bent, from designing new churches. If this is the case, he died a frustrated man, as he built only four new church buildings (two churches and two chapels). His passion is clearly apparent in many other schemes that remained on paper: often no more than a plan, the elevations, a cross-section and perhaps an interior perspective, all beautifully drawn in pen and ink. His first was for Caerhun in 1898 (see pages 24-5). This was followed in 1902 by a reworked (and larger) scheme for the same church, with side aisles, an organ chamber and a vestry on opposite sides of the chancel, and the sanctuary projecting beyond the chancel. Above the chancel arch the cruciform bellcote turned octagonal at the top. Apart from the north porch, the church was symmetrical and abandoned the

relaxed rustic character of the 1898 design. The rounded-head windows of the first design were now pointed: Early English in style rather than Romanesque. It was all rather conventional.

The same conformist atmosphere is apparent in an undated scheme for a 'Mission Church in North Wales near Conway'. The drawings show the nave and chancel sharing a roof which slides down and out over the vestry, echoed by the porch at the other end of the same elevation. A tall bellcote rises above the porch where it meets the nave. The details are, again, conventional, with small trefoiled lights to the side windows, a three-light east window, and an ornate openwork screen dividing the nave and chancel.

In 1910 North entered a competition for a new

church at West Shore, Llandudno. He proposed a squarish plan with wide aisles, each with its own dual-pitched roof, with that of the nave's only just higher than those over the aisles. At each side of the chancel was a chapel, and the chapel at the south-east led, via a vestry/passage, to a twin-gabled church hall, skewed on plan at about 60 degrees to the church to align with the adjacent road. The design is unremarkable, but themes emerge that are hallmarks of North's later churches, for instance the tall, narrow lancets made deeper by mini-buttresses at the east and west gables. The nave's gable windows are triplets and recall the thirteenth-century lancets of Beddgelert church, which North and Hughes's book described as 'possibly the finest architectural feature in the whole of Snowdonia' (Hughes & North 1924: 222). In the event North's entry came second and the competition, judged by the church architect W. D. Caröe, was won by R. T. Beckett.[40] Beckett built a

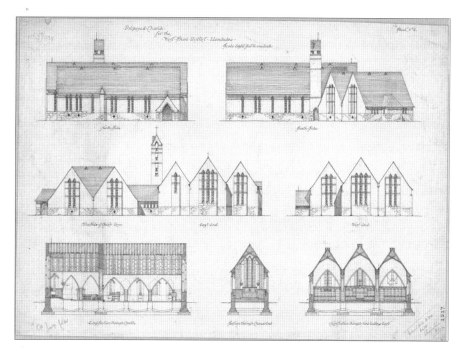

Above. Competition design for St Saviour, West Shore, Llandudno (1910).
RCAHMW, DI2010_0410

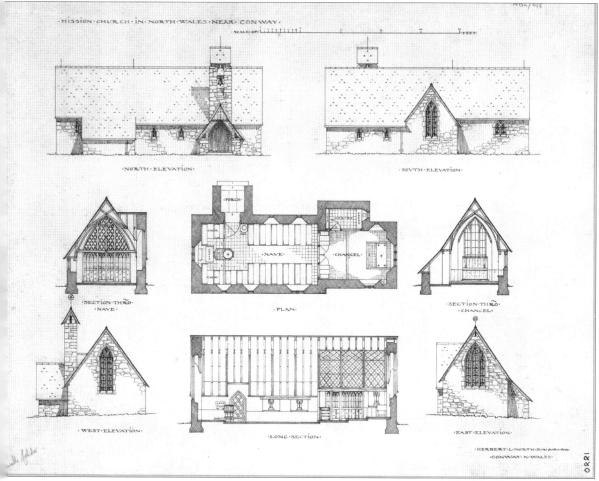

Design for a mission church near Conwy (undated).
RCAHMW, DI2010_0406

*Temporary chapel at
St Winifred's School,
Llanfairfechan (1922).*

*RCAHMW, DI2010_0727,
NPRN 43817*

church using the red Runcorn stone so liked by his master, John Douglas, very different from the granite and roughcast church that North had in mind.

If a small school chapel can be classed as a new church, then North's very first new-build church was the temporary chapel at St Winifred's School, Llanfairfechan, built in 1922. The 'little green Chapel', as the girls called it, had roughcast walls on metal lath and timber frame, a steep roof of asbestos tiles and a strongly-defined structure of scissor trusses connected by cross braces. Daylight was provided by dormers and a large latticed west window recalling the one at Randall Wells' Kempley church, albeit economically done in wood rather than stone. The benches, arranged to face each other, were stained green; the sanctuary was beautifully decorated with Morris hangings and a large embroidery, designed by North, was hung on the east gable above the altar.

This chapel became a prototype for one of three 'Merton Abbey' church types proposed by North for Morris & Co. around 1925.[41] The purpose of the project (which was not a commercial success) was to design and market inexpensive churches and halls 'suited to small or poor parishes, but far superior to that employed in temporary building'. The construction, of 7"x 2" timber sections bolted together, was supposedly based on the medieval

St Edward the Confessor, Kempley, Gloucestershire (Randall Wells, 1902).

Copyright: Brian Edwards. English Heritage. NMR

Cross-section of design for the Merton Abbey churches (c.1925).

RCAHMW, DI2008_1377

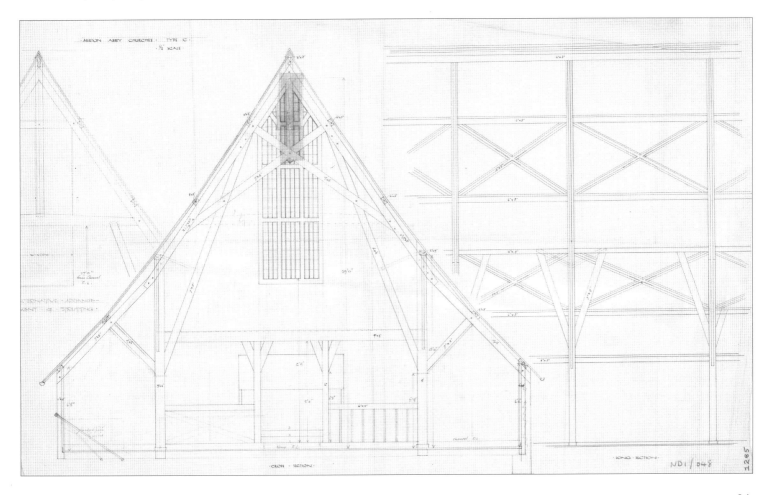

cruck frame. The walls could be of stone, brick or timber-frame and the finishes plain, roughcast or timber boards. Simple church fittings to North's designs could also be purchased, and of course Morris textiles were recommended for the altar frontal, riddel (the curtain behind the altar) and dossal hangings etc.

An opportunity to build a more substantial church arose in 1929 when North was commissioned to design the permanent chapel at St Winifred's School, on the new school site at Plas Llanfair. The result was North's ecclesiastical masterpiece (for its sad demise, see Chapter 5). It was a tall, gaunt building, taking up the north side of a longish quadrangle at the heart of the school.

St Winifred's School chapel, Llanfairfechan (1929-30). The Ida North music wing is on the left.

Adam Voelcker (plan), DI2010_0421, RCAHMW (photograph), NPRN 43817

The entrance was at the west end, through an open porch which was triangular in plan, and then below an arcaded west gallery. At the east end was a pair of tall towers with steep pyramidal roofs and long thin lancet windows reminiscent of Pearson and churches in northern France, though pared down in their decoration. Between them the east end of the chapel terminated in a faceted twin-gable that echoed the diagonal porch. Along the nave and chancel were four, gabled mini-transepts on both sides, alternating at ground level with the lean-to roofs of the slightly raised passage-aisles. The effect of this internally was magical, as one passed alternately from the tall well-lit shafts into the lower, darker spaces. It was an unusual arrangement, chosen perhaps for its spatial drama as well as for the controlled management of daylight, providing good side lighting without the problems of glare as one looked along the nave towards the altar. Did North invent this arrangement, or had he seen it somewhere?

There were two ideas introduced at St Winifred's in combination: the internal buttress (or 'wall-pier') and the passage-aisle. The internal buttress is recognised as originating in southern France in the thirteenth century. It was first seen at the Cordeliers church in Toulouse, then at Albi cathedral (started 1282). The high side walls at Albi required bracing, but buttresses were built on the inside rather than the outside, creating a series of flanking chapels. When a similar plan was used at the Dominican church at Ghent (1240-75) the buttresses were pierced to create a passage-aisle. These two ideas were wholly foreign to medieval English churches. Yet, in the nineteenth century, they became very popular amongst Anglo-Catholic architects, particularly for urban churches. Indeed, Albi and Ghent were brought to the attention of English church architects in contemporary journals:[42] St Augustine, Kilburn (by Pearson, 1870) and St Augustine, Pendlebury (by Bodley & Garner, 1870-4) were early examples of their influence. North would certainly have been aware of these two English churches, and it is quite likely that he would have seen the articles too. Where he appears to break new ground at St Winifred's is the mixing together of the pierced buttresses with the lean-to passage-aisle. It is a combination seen

St Augustine, Pendlebury, Manchester (Bodley and Garner, 1870-4).

Copyright: English Heritage. NMR

Right. Charterhouse School chapel (Giles Gilbert Scott, 1922-7).

Copyright: Jack Jackson. English Heritage. NMR

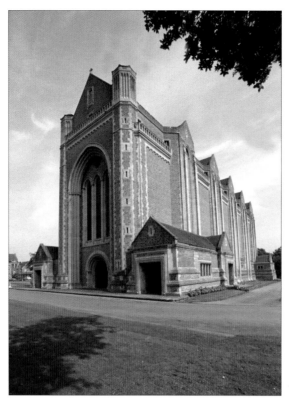

Opposite page. St Winifred's School chapel.

RCAHMW, DI2010_0728, NPRN 43817

Below. St Winifred's School chapel: interior, looking east.

RCAHMW, DI2010_0724, NPRN 43817

rarely. Giles Gilbert Scott, who had used the internal buttress system at Liverpool Cathedral 'to hide the aisle windows when looking down the centre of the cathedral…' (Scott 1953, in Thomas 2002: 29), used a series of mini-transepts and lean-to roofs at his Charterhouse School chapel (1922-7). But it was an earlier church that may have been the real inspiration for North's *parti* at St Winifred's: St Mary, Summerstown, London (by Godfrey Pinkerton, 1903-4). Though stylistically very different, it had the alternating arrangement of mini-transepts and lean-to roofs, and the paired arcade arches which North adopted. The church was published in *Recent English Ecclesiastical Architecture* and North had a copy of this book in his library (Nicholson & Spooner, c.1911).

The chapel was built of roughcast-covered concrete bricks that were 'made from the stone of the mountain quarry [at Penmaenmawr] and were manufactured at its foot. The floor is of the same granite […]. Half-a-dozen or so of the oldest and most highly-skilled workmen were entrusted with the selection of these blocks by the quarry manager, whose two daughters were at St Winifred's'

THE CHAPEL, ST WINIFRED'S SCHOOL, LLANFAIRFECHAN   W 7680

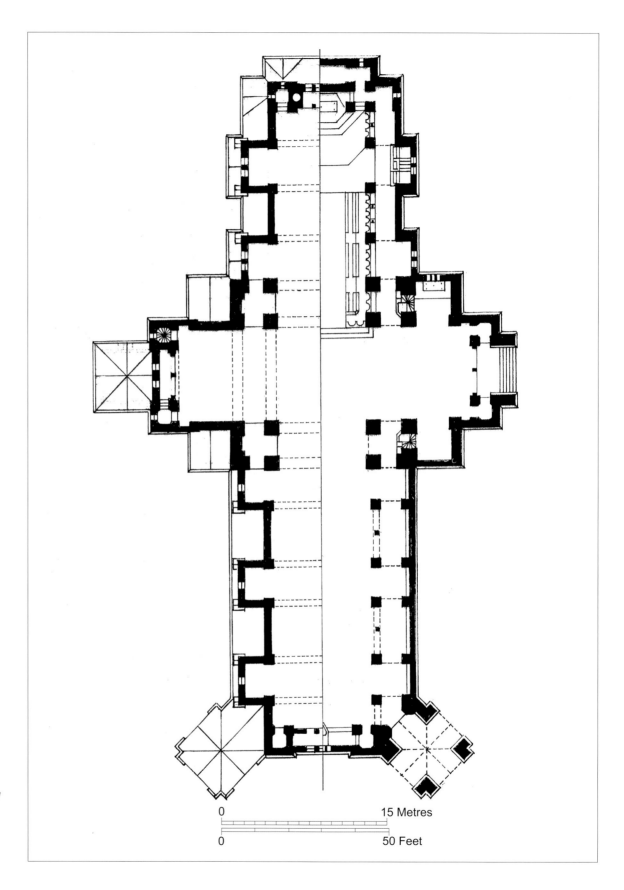

Plan of competition entry for Guildford cathedral (1930). Upper level on left, floor level on right.

Adam Voelcker, DI2010_0420

0   15 Metres

0   50 Feet

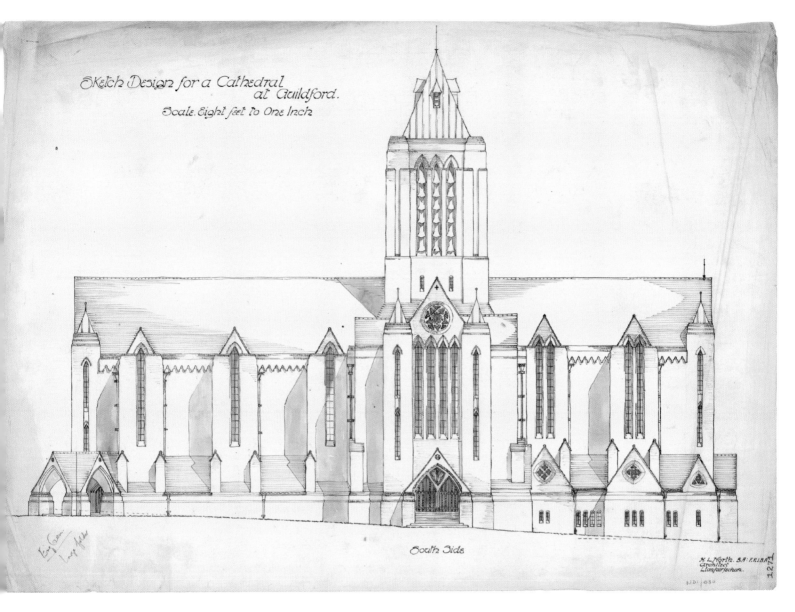

Sketch Design for a Cathedral
at Guildford.
Scale. Eight feet to One Inch

South Side

(Roberts 1937: 40). Not so true to the Arts and Crafts ethic were the asbestos roof tiles, laid diagonally and chosen perhaps for economy. The internal walls and soaring transverse arches were of exposed brick, painted off-white. The underside of the steep roof was decorated in cobalt, green oxide and vermilion, and depicted one of North's favourite themes, the Heavenly City. The benches were made of American walnut and faced each other across the church, college-fashion. In the lofty sanctuary, sitting like a jewel in a casket, was the altar, covered and backed by Morris hangings and sheltering below an ornate baldacchino canopy worthy of Wilson or Comper.

Shortly afterwards, in 1930, North developed these same ideas further and on a grander scale when, along with 160 other architects, he entered a competition to design the new cathedral in Guildford. His entry proposed a crossing tower with a ceremonial south transeptal entrance mirrored on the north by a small chapter-house. The chancel and sanctuary were like a miniature St Winifred's chapel, though with vestries in the basement. At the west end further entrances were at the two corners, placed on the diagonal with cross-gabled porch roofs above each. The same arrangement of alternating mini-transepts and lean-to passage-aisles was adopted, scaled up to

Proposed south elevation Guildford cathedral.

RCAHMW, DI2008_1364

87

cathedral proportions. Progressing along the passage-aisle would have been an exhilarating experience, heightened by the dramatic crossing space almost at mid-point along the cathedral's length. But the exterior appearance of North's design is a disappointment. The steep gables and thin towers, the elongated lancets with pointed heads, and the play with diagonals are all familiar,

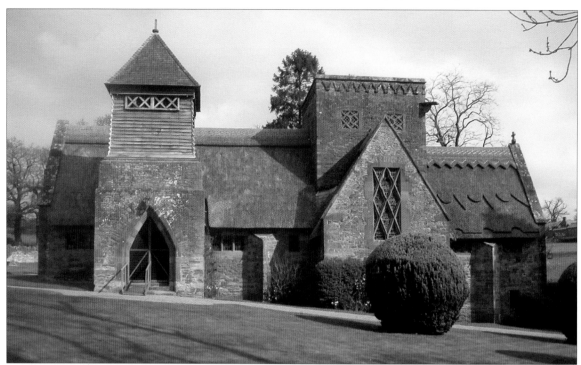

All Saints, Brockhampton (William Lethaby, 1902).

Adam Voelcker

St Andrew, Roker (Prior, 1904-7).

RIBA Edwin Smith. Library Photographs Collection

but they somehow lack conviction when magnified. North must have realised this for there was an attempt to relieve the vast areas of brindled brick and Ham Hill stone with Gothic decoration. There is a trefoil corbel-table at the upper eaves level and tracery to some of the windows and doorways. The detail is all rather conventional, however, and certainly lacks the originality and power of detail seen at early twentieth-century churches such as Lethaby's All Saints, Brockhampton (1902) and Prior's St Andrew, Roker (1904-7). St Winifred's chapel was more convincing, too, leading one to conclude either that North tempered his details to what he thought might be expected by the Dean and Chapter, or, more likely, he was daunted by the sheer scale. In the event, there was no winner. A second, limited competition was held two years later and the five entries were published in *The Architect and Building News* in July 1932.[43] It is interesting that two of the designs had alternating high mini-transepts and low passage-aisles, similar to North's. The winning design, a very polished and convincing entry by Edward Maufe, had a central tower and was an essay in reworked and pared-down Gothic: a more modern Gothic than North's.

North returned to the small scale with his next job, a chapel for the Church Hostel in Bangor,

Left. Aisle arch and west front, Guildford cathedral (Edward Maufe, begun 1936).

Adam Voelcker

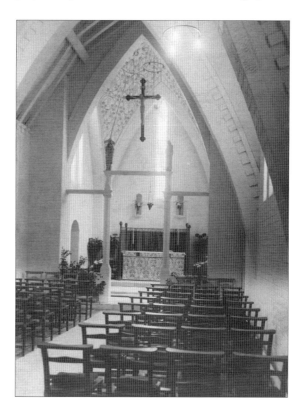

Church Hostel chapel, Bangor (1933). Early photograph, showing the original screen and altar.

DI2010_0733, NPRN 25997

commissioned in 1933 by its warden, the Revd Glyn Simon, whom North had known at St Winifred's. It is an intimate building, divided into four structural bays by steep brick arches which spring from low down. The chancel's roof lifts to become a cross-gabled vault over the space, rather similar to the baldacchino in St Winifred's chapel, its underside painted with a pattern of green vines on a blue trellis. A simple open screen (since removed) symbolically divided this from the small nave.

The same structural arrangement, a series of steeply pointed transverse arches, was used again when he designed the church of The Holy Spirit, Harlescott, built in around 1936 for a fast-growing suburb of Shrewsbury. It survives but is now much changed, in use as a community centre. At this church the series of five arches supports a green pantiled roof, which sweeps low to the nave eaves and then extends even lower, over the north and south porches at the west end, and over the two

Church Hostel chapel, Bangor. Chancel ceiling, with east window by F. C. Eden.
RCAHMW, DS2010_664_009, NPRN 25997

Opposite. Church Hostel chapel, Bangor.
RCAHMW, DS2010_664_006, NPRN 25997

Church of the Holy Spirit,
Harlescott, Shrewsbury
(1934-36): interior, looking
east (early photograph).
DI2010-0399

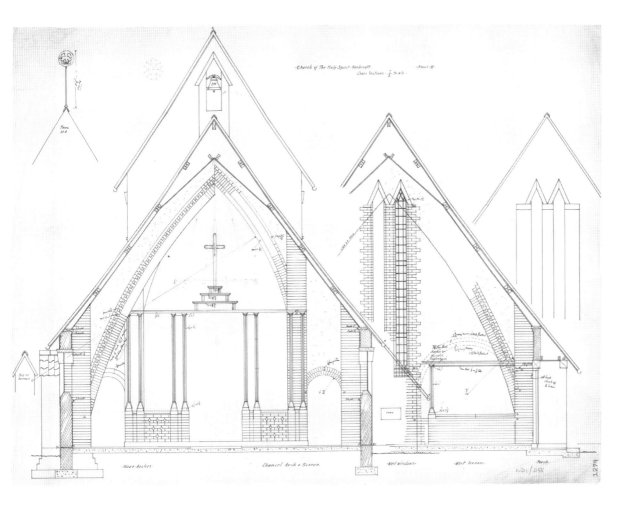

Harlescott church: cross-section and plan.
RCAHMW, DI2008_1374

vestries at the east end. The vestry roofs bifurcate about the long axis, appearing as a pair of gables on the east elevation and clasping the base of a pantile-roofed tower which rises high above the chancel. The fenestration is reduced to simplicity itself, the basic window component a narrow lancet with a triangular head protected by a projecting canted hood, also triangular – North often used this feature, which is reminiscent of Prior's detailing at St Andrew, Roker, Sunderland (inspired by the Saxon work at St Peter, Barton-on-Humber). The nave is lit by groups of six lancets, the vestries by groups of five, the tower by groups of seven with a single elongated lancet in the tower's west wall.

The angularity of the exterior at Harlescott was somewhat softened by the graceful curves of the transverse brick arches, which marched down the nave. In the sanctuary light poured down from the high-level windows in the tower, in contrast to the dark nave, a trick North must have learnt from Lethaby's church at Brockhampton. The interior was painted off-white; it was free of decoration and detail apart from some sparse floral patterns painted on the underside of the roof. The altar and riddel stood below the east window; in front of the choir was a simple open screen with rood above. The

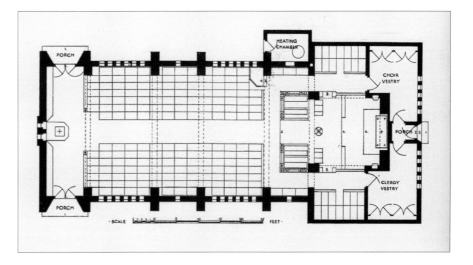

93

All Saints, Brockhampton (Lethaby, 1902).

Adam Voelcker

St Catherine, Blackwell, Worcestershire (1939-41).
RCAHMW, DS2010_030_004

chancel and sanctuary nestled between the north and south vestries, which were linked behind the sanctuary by a short passage and external doorway; the plan of the east end was remarkably like the 'Plan for a Modern Chancel' illustrated in Dearmer's *The Parson's Handbook* (1921: 85).[44]

The transverse, or diaphragm, arch system seems to have been used early by Prior at Holy Trinity, Bothenhampton, Dorset in 1884. Prior used it again, to greater effect and in conjunction with passage-aisles, at Roker church. Lethaby chose this form for Brockhampton church where the arch shape is particularly distinctive, taking the form almost of an equilateral triangle with its two sides just slightly curved. It is a modern interpretation of the Gothic arch, stripped of its historical associations and taken back to the fundamental essence of two members propped against each other to span a space. North used this very shape and for similar reasons. He had loved it from years back (he first used it for the inglenook archway at Bolnhurst in 1899) and saw an opportunity to use it in the appropriate setting of a church. He was not alone in this pursuit of a contemporary church style rooted in Gothic principles. Around the same time W. Curtis Green was designing churches whose interiors could almost be mistaken for North's own (for example St Christopher, Cove, Hampshire and St George, Waddon, Surrey). A glance at two Incorporated Church Building Society (ICBS) publications that featured recent churches in the 1930s (Harlescott is among them) shows that this arch shape was adopted fairly frequently (ICBS 1936, 1947). The more severe examples are reminiscent of German churches built earlier in the century (such as St Apollinaris, Freilingsdorf, by Dominikus Böhm, 1926-7).

In many respects North's second (and last) full-scale church to be built, St Catherine, Blackwell, Worcestershire, was a stylistic step backward from

Opposite. Blackwell church: interior, looking east.
RCAHMW, DS2010_030_004

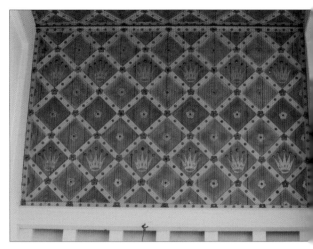

Blackwell church: south elevation, interior and detail of chancel ceiling.

RCAHMW, DS2010_030_006 (top left), DS2010_030_012 (left), DS2010_030_021 (above)

Harlescott. It was begun in 1939, was completed just before North's death in 1941, and was largely financed by the Earl of Plymouth and Edward Grey, of Grey's Department Store in Birmingham.[45] Its plan is more traditional than Harlescott, with an aisled nave, a projecting sanctuary and a north vestry. The detail, too, is more traditional: there is a big rose window at the west end and a wagon-roof with a dentilated cornice at wall-head height. The arcade arches are moulded and meet the plain piers at an angle rather than die into them seamlessly. Alan Brooks calls the church 'Scandinavian-looking' (Brooks 2007: 153). Paradoxically, it is also traditionally English in a way that Harlescott is not. One feels at Harlescott that an individual new style had begun to take shape, but at Blackwell there was a loss of nerve.

Rough sketches for the very last church project North worked on may elucidate this. One of the designs for a chapel at St Michael's College, Llandaff, looks conventional enough on plan and appears to be designed to fit an existing site, presumably the college (where George Pace was later to design the chapel).[46] But a perspective of a different design, supposedly for St Michael's yet set isolated in mountain scenery, shows an extraordinary building, almost futurist in character. Though it also has familiar North features, it suggests he was exploring new territory in terms of his formal vocabulary (Hilling 1975:94).

Design for St Michael,
Llandaff, Cardiff (undated).
RCAHMW, DI2010_0730,
NPRN 31889

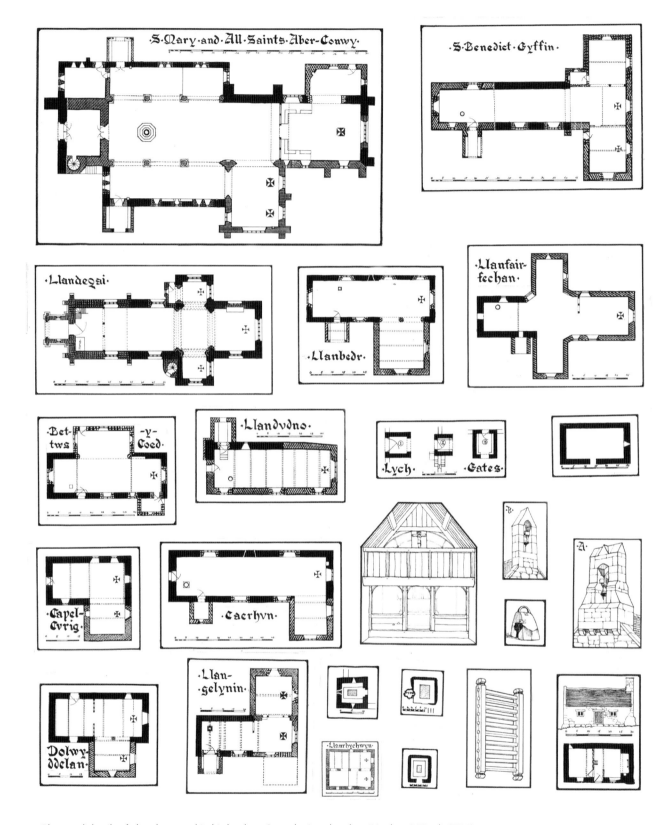

Plans and details of churches, used in his book on Snowdonian churches (Hughes & North 1924).

North was passionately involved with church work during his entire career, from his 1898 Caerhun project right up to his death in 1941 – indeed, even his summer holidays were tours around Britain looking at churches.[47] The span is even greater if his early interest at school is included. How did he develop during these sixty years and what did he achieve?

North's upbringing surrounded him with churches old and new. There is no doubt about the value he placed on the medieval ones. Where the newer churches were concerned, he would have seen these as following a tradition, in other words to be dressed in the Gothic style, which he believed was the only style appropriate for churches.

His High Church upbringing instilled in him a set of liturgical beliefs, which were confirmed and strengthened by his early involvement with Sedding and Wilson and by his adherence to Dearmer and *The Parson's Handbook*. These were put into practice, largely through the Church Crafts League, at his early projects for church fittings and decoration; but ideas were beginning to change as the twentieth century dawned. Theological reformers across Europe were reassessing the role of the Church in society, giving birth to the Liturgical Movement, whose aim was to make the laity active participants rather than passive spectators. At the same time a few architects were beginning to question the role

Unexecuted design for 'A Simple Suburban Church' (1937).
RCAHMW, DI2008_1367

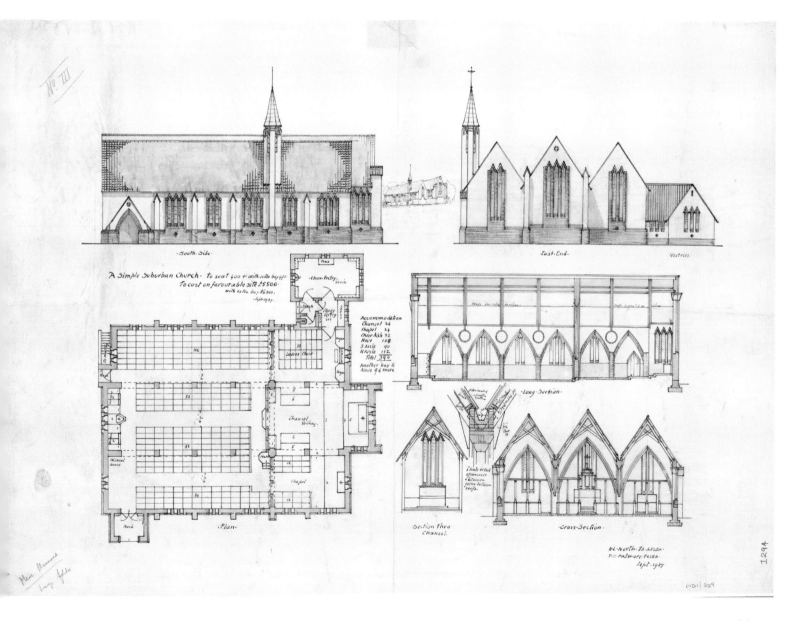

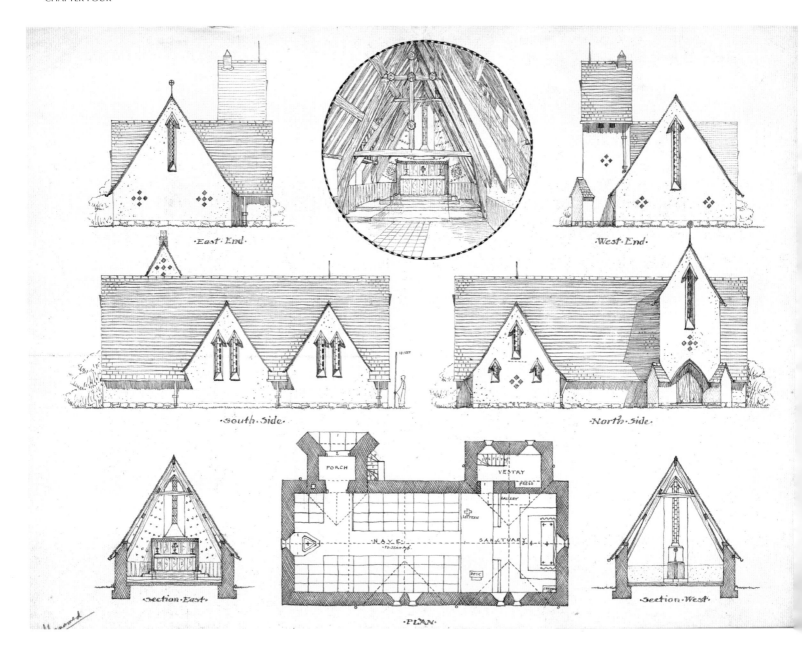

·East·End·

·West·End·

·South·Side·

·North·Side·

·Section·East·

PORCH

VESTRY

PRESS

GALLERY

NAVE·
·TO·SEAT·176·

SANCTUARY

·Section·West·

·PLAN·

Design for an unidentified church (undated).
RCAHMW, DI2008_1279

of architecture in the modern world. The parallel implication was that the liturgical layout of churches was outdated. Chancel arches and screens shut out the laity, and beautiful fittings were as irrelevant as the historicist styles in which churches were clothed. Both Lethaby and Prior were aware of this shift. Lethaby wrote: 'The modern way of building must be flexible and vigorous, even smart and hard. We must give up designing the broken-down picturesque which is part of the ideal of make-believe.' (Lethaby 1911, in Davey 1995: 70). Prior criticised

church building for its 'trivial efforts of traditional picturesqueness'. Both men designed churches, but whether they put their theories convincingly into practice is a moot point. On one hand, both Brockhampton and Roker can be seen as churches fitting perfectly into the Gothic tradition, with even a degree of the picturesque, particularly at the former. On the other hand, it can be argued that both were modern buildings of their time, taking advantage of the latest building materials and techniques and avoiding the question of style.

Clues about North's attitudes at this time can be gleaned from his book on Welsh churches and the few church building projects he did before the First World War: his 1902 Caerhun design and the competition entry for West Shore church (1910). *The Old Churches of Arllechwedd*, written by North in 1906 (preceding *The Old Churches of Snowdonia* written with Harold Hughes in 1908), is a eulogy to the type of small medieval country church that survived in north Wales, often remarkably intact, interspersed with an occasional implication about contemporary church design. Much of his praise is romantic and is based on how well the old churches sit in the landscape, but sometimes there are insights into how the churches must have fulfilled their liturgical obligations. For instance, of Gyffin church he says: 'There can be little doubt that the medieval altar stood away from the east wall under the four centre panels of the vault representing the four mystic symbols, a much more dignified position than the usual one at the present day, against the east wall.' (North 1906: 50). Not only is there a suggestion here that he knew of Lethaby's *Architecture, Mysticism and Myth* (1891), but it is clear that he interpreted churches as more than charming objects in the countryside but rather as buildings with function and meaning. When he put his thoughts onto paper with the Caerhun and West Shore designs he certainly had function in mind, but there were no progressive ideas, either in the liturgical layout or in the architecture. Both schemes were firmly rooted in the past, with medieval plans, no doubt beautiful fittings (had they been executed) and recognisably Gothic elevations. There is just a hint that the literal Gothic detail of the Caerhun design was stripped down in the West Shore church, suggesting that North, too, was wondering if a more modern style might not be appropriate as the new century rolled on.

Liturgical reform continued after the First World War. It is not clear whether North was aware of developments abroad during the 1920s and 1930s, particularly in Germany where the modern liturgy seemed to be evolving hand in hand with the Modern Movement in architecture. North's views on Modernist buildings are not recorded, but it is probable that he disliked them intensely.[48] Their flat roofs and cuboid shapes were far removed from his beloved Gothic, and even if their interiors were plain, they did not work as foils to the jewels inside since the jewels were even plainer. In Britain Father Gabriel Hebert's *Liturgy and Society* had a significant impact. Written in 1935, it gave birth to the Parish Communion movement, replacing Mattins with the Eucharist as the main Sunday service and generally involving the laity as participants rather than as onlookers.

The effect of liturgical reform on church design in Britain was fairly minimal, as Peter Hammond points out in *Liturgy and Architecture* (1960), and as can be seen in the Incorporated Church Building Society publications. Most modern churches built in Britain between 1928 and 1940 were based on traditional plans and were clothed in a variety of historicist styles, the first of three categories Hammond uses for classifying modern churches. The second category included those that were made to look modern (like a power-station or a cinema, which was at least preferable to aping the past) but did not answer the brief in terms of church function. Only a handful provided a suitable setting for modern worship, his third and most important category.[49] North's post-war churches would presumably fit somewhere between the first two categories, with his design for Guildford cathedral and Blackwell church firmly in the first. His design for 'A Simple Suburban Church' of 1937, an exact reworking of his West Shore design of almost three decades earlier, would also be included here. Harlescott church strays into the middle category, its Gothic style so reduced that it becomes almost modern. Nothing is liturgically new in these churches however (apart from the chancel screens being more open and minimalist than in his earlier churches). Such considerations would have been irrelevant to North, rooted by his Anglo-Catholic upbringing and training. For him, gorgeous fittings and vestments, beautiful ceremony and sweet plainsong were far more to the point than engaging in participatory worship. Thus North, despite his small forays into experimentation, was one of a group of church architects who, like J. N. Comper, F. C. Eden, C. A. Nicholson and others, upheld the conservative tradition of church-building well into the twentieth century.

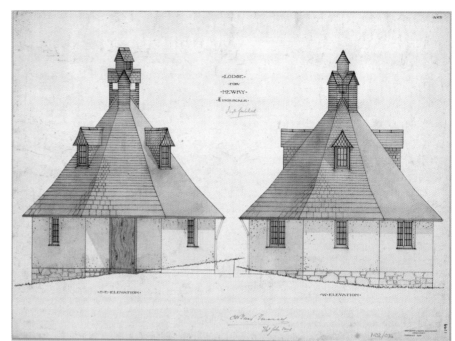

Lodge at Newry (later Plas Heulog) (1907).

RCAHMW, DI2010_0408 (right),

DI2008_1266 (below)

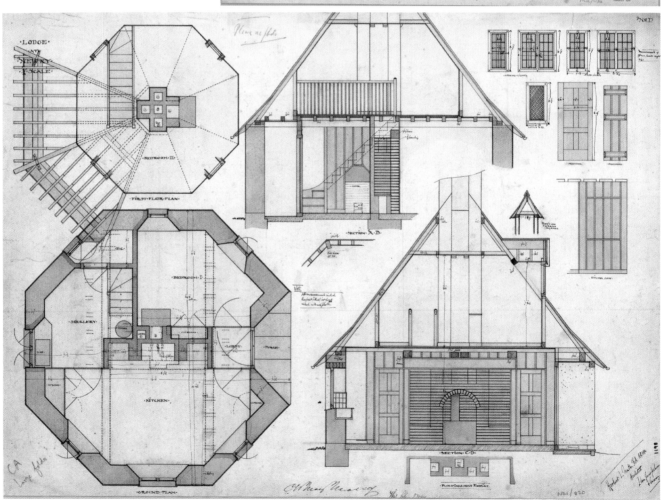

Other Work

North occasionally designed buildings that were neither churches nor houses. Two early jobs were the church hall at Caerhun and the school at Gyffin, Conwy, both built about 1902-3. The hall commission came about as a result of North's mother riding over one day to Caerhun and offering the vicar £100 on condition that her son would be the architect.[50] It was an enlargement of an existing parish room and enclosed the increased accommodation below an intriguing roof, which swept up from the familiar pair of gables to a gabled bell turret.

'A little extreme, my dear fellow, a little extreme' is how North described it to his assistant R. S. Nickson.[51] Equally inventive is the three-sided coal-house in the garden, with its three-sided pyramidal roof.

The National (church) school at Gyffin is more conventional. The roof is straightforward and the bell-turret just a slated fleche. Good daylighting is provided by big gable windows similar to those used in the County schools of the period.[52] A very full set of drawings for this building survives in the National Monuments Record of Wales, with huge

Church hall, Caerhun (1902-3). RCAHMW, DS2010_673_002, NPRN 407862

School, Gyffin (1902-3).
RCAHMW, DI2005_1217,
NPRN 96659

watercoloured elevations and constructional details. Even the latrine block in the garden is given love and attention.

The lodge North designed in 1907 at Newry (later Plas Heulog), Llanfairfechan, must be mentioned because, though small, it is delightful. It is octagonal in plan, with the scullery, the kitchen and a bedroom all sharing the central stack that rises up through the second bedroom to a busy flourish of gabled flues at the apex of the steep slated roof. Surprisingly, Lawrence Weaver did not feature this gem in the chapter on lodges in the third edition of his book on cottages (Weaver 1926).

More substantial is the Church Institute, Llanfairfechan, built 1911-12. This is a building of real quality and is remarkably unchanged. The site was donated by North's mother; Herbert gave his professional services free and tended the little garden. The building was designed as a village hall, with a stage at one end, the hall at the other and a small kitchen off the hall. There are entrances at each end, through little, low wings which are set at 60 degrees to the main volume and contain the lavatories. The interior is plain but not without charm. A green-stained timber dado lines the main spaces, and a brick Gothic fireplace adorns the end

wall of the hall. The external walls are roughcast and the steep, all-embracing roof is covered with small, greenish slates laid to diminishing courses. The tall windows are small-paned and leaded and are set back within openings with Gothic heads. North was pragmatic about formal issues such as symmetry. Whereas many Arts and Crafts architects eschewed symmetry because it smacked of classical formalism, North was quite happy if it served his purposes. (Of North's roughly sixty identifiable houses, about two-thirds are asymmetrical in elevation. This still leaves twenty or so which are not, showing that North was happy enough with the formality which symmetry entailed). At the Institute he took a relaxed middle approach. There is symmetry about the mirrored entrance porches either side of the main volume but such symmetry is happily pushed aside by the different volumetric and level requirements of the plan and section. This is Gothic in the true Pugin sense.

Church Institute, Llanfairfechan (1911-12).

RCAHMW, DS2007_401_003 (above), DI2010_0427 (plan), Adam Voelcker, NPRN 471

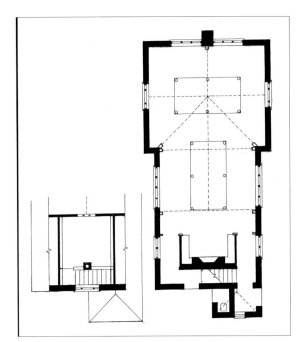

Churchmen's Club, Llanfairfechan (1926).

Adam Voelcker (plan), DI2010_0423, RCAHMW (photograph), DS2010_659_001, NPRN 409914

Next door is the Churchmen's Club, similar in many ways, though smaller and built some years later, in 1926. Again, the site was donated, this time by North himself (his mother had died in 1917) and, again, he gave his services free. He also lent £700 on condition the work was carried out by his own team of men. (North liked to use builders he knew. Frank Tyldesley, who built many of North's houses in the 1930s, recalled that North preferred not to go out to tender on jobs, relying on negotiation or plain, simple trust.)[53] The building consists of a large lofty room, with a fireplace in an inglenook at one end that is overlooked through a tiny shuttered window from the upstairs library. The entrance is from a passage alongside the ingle, mirrored by a narrow kitchen on the far side. In essence, the plan is like the hall portion of the sort of artistic houses that Baillie Scott was designing earlier in the century.

Cottage Hospital, Dolgellau
(1929).

RCAHMW, DS2010_662_007,
NPRN 409686

A year or so later North designed the Dolgellau and Barmouth District Cottage Hospital in Dolgellau. This had been founded in 1920 in a converted house; the lease expired in 1928, so funds were raised locally and North's new building opened in 1929. It was then enlarged by him in 1933 and is now much altered and engulfed by new buildings. The original entrance was at the fork of a Y-plan wing of three storeys, up a flight of steps and through a typically 'Northesque' Gothic archway. From here the main corridor continued on axis towards a long cross-wing, with the men's ward on one side and the women's on the other (by this point single-storey as the building is on a hill). The formal vocabulary of the building is not very different from that of North's houses. The slate roofs, roughcast walls and tall small-paned windows are all familiar, though a certain civic formality has crept in. Whether it was the right

decision to employ a domestic and church architect to design a hospital was perhaps a moot point. Certainly the ethos behind the design of cottage hospitals encouraged architects to 'conform as nearly as possible to the character of the neighbouring cottages' (*The Builder*, 29th February 1898: 145) and Ian Allan says that the local people liked its homely quality, but at least one staff member was less enthusiastic about some of its practical aspects and its 'wasteful affectations'.[54]

There is sadly nothing to see of St Winifred's School, Llanfairfechan, as it was demolished in 1970. The school was North's biggest and most constant employer, giving him commissions from 1922 through to 1937. 'Employer' is perhaps not the entirely appropriate term, as North (who was known as 'Pa North' by the children) was deeply intertwined in the life and running of the school and gave or loaned large amounts of money

St Winifred's School, Llanfairfechan: Dean Roberts Hall (1929-30). The Ida North music wing is to the left, the classroom wing to the right.

RCAHMW, DI2010_0726, NPRN 23250

towards its buildings. (The total debt on the buildings in the mid-1930s was £14,400; over £11,000 of this was owed to North. Pam Phillips confirms that her grandfather was never very good with money when it was his own.)

St Winifred's School was founded in 1887 in Bangor by the Hon. Eleanor Douglas Pennant as a school for girls, under the aegis of the Midland Division of the Woodard Schools.[55] In 1922 it moved to Llanfairfechan, taking up residence first at Plas Gwyn, off Station Road, then in 1924 at North's home, Plas Llanfair (when he moved back to Wern Isaf). North's first new buildings for the school were the temporary chapel (*see* Chapter 4) and a classroom wing, built in 1922. The chapel was taken down in 1930 and was later re-erected

St Winifred's School, classroom wing (1929-30).

RCAHMW, DI2010_0725, NPRN 23250

at a girls' school in Southport, Lancashire. The classroom wing was of similar construction. It had gabled cross-wings each end of a three-bay wing with tall dormer windows that extended as far above the eaves as they did below. Above the gable windows were areas of tiled diaper-work.

Once the school moved to its new site, it could expand. A new classroom wing was built around 1925 and extended in 1929-30 when the Dean Roberts Hall, the Ida North Music Wing and the new chapel were also built (see Chapter 4). They formed a quadrangle, with the chapel (with music wing beyond) on the north-west side, the hall on the short north-east side and the long classroom wing facing the chapel across the courtyard. The classrooms were linked by a glazed cloister walkway on the inner side, the inspiration clearly collegiate. On the other side of the wing big windows provided sunlight to the classrooms and diaper work decorated the gables, similar to the first classroom building at Plas Gwyn. The interiors of the classrooms and hall were flooded with daylight and enlivened by the scissor trusses which were the characteristic feature of North's Merton Abbey designs.

A large sanatorium was added in 1933. It stood apart from the other buildings and had a bent, sun-trap plan reminiscent of Wern Isaf. Large gables faced the sea, with wide, slightly curved verge boards that were untypical of North and somehow gave the building a Germanic flavour.

Further buildings at St Winifred's were planned by North, including a large dormitory and dining-hall block, but the outbreak of the Second World War halted expansion, and by the time the war was over North was dead. The school was closed in 1967 and demolished in 1970 to make way for a housing estate. This was a tragedy of the first order as the school was a substantial and impressive part of North's *oeuvre*, and the chapel was perhaps his masterpiece. Before the school was demolished the east side of Llanfairfechan must have been a remarkable place with the cloistered college at its centre, the Church Institute and Churchmen's Club nearby, the Close of houses on the hillside behind and, in the distance, the two village churches. All the new buildings were dressed in North's distinctive modern Gothic style, and as an ensemble it must have been the nearest North ever came to recreating the physical counterpart of his vision of an ideal medieval society, perhaps the Heavenly City which he portrayed in his church decoration schemes.

St Winifred's School, interior of the Dean Roberts Hall.
RCAHMW, DI2010_0723

*St Peter's church,
Penrhosgarnedd, Bangor (1956).*

*RCAHMW, DS2010_665_001 (right),
DS2010_665_002 (below),
NPRN 411861*

North's Legacy

Herbert North's legacy lies both in his buildings and the practices that he passed on to followers, directly or indirectly. He employed assistants who became architects in their own right, though none developed national reputations. R. S. Nickson, grandson of the John Nickson who had commissioned Cefn Isaf from North, was a colourful character who, after wavering between a future as a professional pianist or architect, chose the latter career. He had trained at Cambridge and the Architectural Association in London and may have had two spells with North, one about 1932 when he was engaged largely with his own projects under North's guidance. One of his own churches, St Chad, Bolton, was featured in the Incorporated Church Building Society publication *Fifty New Churches* in 1947. He also designed church fittings.

Perceval Mitchell Padmore (1896-1992) joined North as an assistant in 1924 and became his partner in 1926: strictly speaking North's post-1926 buildings were by the firm 'North and Padmore' even though some drawings named only North. Padmore also became North's son-in-law, marrying Ida Joan, and although this may have brought the two men closer on the domestic front, their professional relationship was not entirely without friction – North was an exacting man and liked things to be done his own way.[56] In 1936 Padmore applied for the post of County Architect in Oxfordshire. North was reasonable about terminating their partnership and wrote him a very fair letter of recommendation, but in the event Padmore decided to stay put. When North died in 1941 Padmore continued working under the firm's joint name, sometimes designing very North-like churches, such as Penrhosgarnedd (1950), sometimes designing ones that were rather different, as at Benllech (1964). Ironically, given

Herbert and Ida North in old age, below Wern Isaf.
RCAHMW, DI2009_1382, Courtesy of Pamela J. Phillips

North's passion for churches, Padmore had more opportunities to design churches in Wales, particularly as he was surveyor to the Bangor Diocese in the 1950s-60s, yet he could not match North's design flair and imagination.

Padmore was joined by Frank Dann about 1965. A link can be made between North and the firm that Dann later established with Stewart Powell Bowen and Bill Davies (Bowen Dann Davies), which has undertaken some of the best modern buildings in north Wales. Their work is characterised by expansive slate roofs that slide and cascade like landscapes and often sweep low at the eaves, by white roughcast walls (of a yet more textured type than North's) and dark-stained timber windows. These do not look like North's buildings, yet they share a simplicity and unpretentiousness that would have appealed to North. They look rooted in their settings; indeed one can recognise in the use of local materials and forms the evolution of the modern Welsh vernacular that North had begun.

How far was North conscious of establishing a modern Welsh vernacular? He certainly admired the way traditional Welsh buildings sat happily in the landscape and used the local materials. He attempted, with a measure of success, to emulate this with his own buildings. Walls were built of local stone, or of bricks made locally, and roofs were covered with Welsh slates. North Wales was not known for any particularly fine craft traditions in building, so North kept detail simple. He liked using familiar builders and was content to repeat well-tested details rather than reinvent each project, and yet his style was not exclusively 'Welsh'. When he built elsewhere in Britain the formal language he adopted was usually the same as that of his buildings in Wales. The house he built in about 1931 for a doctor in Higher Bebington, Cheshire, is very little different from those he was building in north Wales at the same time and even uses rustic diminished course roof slates, probably from Wales. His design for a cottage at Shenstone, Staffordshire (1912) is more or less a repeat of Whilome, Llanfairfechan. Blackwell church, in the leafy suburbs of Bromsgrove, is exactly the sort of church he would have designed for a rural parish in Snowdonia. The roofs are not of slate and the roughcast walls are brick rather than stone, but otherwise the style is that of his Welsh church projects.

The house at 28 Jack Straw's Lane, Headington,

Oxford, looks as if it might be a slight concession to its context. There is something not quite typical of North in the details: the clay-tiled roof, the leaded-light windows and the large hipped dormer. A surviving drawing of 'a house for H. Smith Esq at Headington', dated 1926, shows a similar plan and a similar disposition of exterior elements, but all in the familiar style of his Welsh houses. If this is the same house, it is intriguing to speculate whether he adjusted the design before (or as) it was built, or whether its execution was in fact the result of the builder changing the details. After all, Oxford was a long way for North to travel in order to supervise the building work. Perhaps only at Keldwith do we see a conscious effort outside north Wales to build in a way rooted in the local vernacular. His usual gables give the house its unmistakable North appearance, but for once the walls are not roughcast and there is a hint that North was relishing the use of local limestone and non-Welsh slate.

So, on the whole, North was always tempted to follow his own formal language and his preferred palette of materials, as Voysey did, rather than adopt and develop the local vernacular when working away from home. He was happiest with what was familiar to him.

Nor was North an architect who let his designs develop freely. He was not inclined to let the creative process take him where it would; he was too straight-laced for that. Much as he admired Lethaby, he was unable to indulge in an *Architecture of Adventure*[57] and 'give up hugging the coasts of the known, to sail forth boldly under the stars' (Lethaby 1910). When Lethaby wrote 'The modern way of building must be flexible and vigorous, even smart and hard. We must give up designing the broken-down picturesque which is part of the ideal of make believe'(Lethaby 1911, in Davey 1995: 70), North might well have agreed. His version of the picturesque could never be described as 'make believe' and his logical approach to creating functional forms was inventive, but he could not break out of his style of building, so firmly founded in his own personality, to put such thoughts into action.

The 'modern way of building' was an issue with which North had to come to terms in one way or another, and it is interesting to put him and his later work into the context of Britain and the Continent in the 1920s to 1940s. This context has been succinctly described by Alan Powers (2007:

Chapter 1), who shows how, as new technology such as reinforced concrete, steel framing and plate glass developed, continental architects embraced it, whereas in Britain most architects disguised it, if they adopted it at all. Lethaby wanted to attach a 'laboratory of building' to every school of architecture as early as 1904 but was overruled by the classicists who were more interested in *beaux-arts* planning and the latest developments in America. In 1914 the radically influential Deutsche Werkbund exhibition was held in Cologne. Lethaby visited this, presumably seeing buildings such as Walter Gropius's Model

Factory and Bruno Taut's Glass Pavilion. In 1917 the Building Research Establishment was established in Britain and after the end of the First World War new technology was harnessed to ease the housing shortage. The year 1927 saw the translation into English of Le Corbusier's *Vers une Architecture* and the completion of the experimental Weissenhof estate near Stuttgart, co-ordinated by Mies van der Rohe – both contemporary with North's Seiriol Road housing in Bangor.

The Congrès Internationaux d'Architecture Moderne (CIAM) was founded in 1928; the Minimum

Plas Menai, Y Felinheli (by Bowen Dann Davies, 1982).

RCAHMW, DS2007_413_004, NPRN 406861

Dwelling was the subject of its 1929 conference in Frankfurt and the International Style the subject in New York in 1932. The innovative architectural partnership, Tecton, was founded in Britain in 1932. In the slump of the late 1920s and early 1930s there was little work for architects, so entering competitions was attractive: competitions for Guildford Cathedral, the RIBA headquarters in Portland Place and Norwich Town Hall were all held in 1932. In 1934 the Dudley Report suggested that the cost of large-scale housing could be reduced to well below any previous level of cost by rationalised organisation and carefully studied design. Where did North, who was temperamentally old-fashioned, sit in this context and how much did he embrace advances in building technology?

It has already been suggested that North's keenness on economy might have attracted him to the Minimum Dwelling research being carried out on the Continent. He might have taken modern materials and construction techniques more seriously to heart had his innate conservatism not got in the way. After the First World War he did use modern materials. He used concrete brick cavity walls, and he specified factory-made metal casement windows instead of handmade timber ones. Although he used Vita glass (for health-giving reasons as its new formulation was designed to bring ultraviolet light into interiors), he still kept to the small-pane cottage-casement style of his pre-war windows. He rarely, if ever, used steel beams in his domestic buildings as the spans were short. In his churches there was usually the height to use tall Gothic arches of brick, or he would bolt together pieces of timber to form trusses, as at his Merton Abbey buildings.[58] He used concrete less reluctantly as time went by. For economy, and to help control dampness, he designed concrete rafts for the combined floors and foundations of his Seiriol Road houses (1927). Faced with the huge structure of his Guildford Cathedral competition design (1930), he resorted to concrete vaults to support the roof and concrete ring-beams for the towers. However, it was only very late on that he appears to have accepted concrete expressed honestly rather than concealed: the precast rose window and the chancel screen at Blackwell church (1939-41) are examples. Even so, he had difficulty in drawing his flat-roofed housing scheme

of 1940 in its wartime mode (that is, before the pitched-roof upper storey was added, for peacetime use) (page 72).

Herein lies the essence of North's dilemma: ethically he accepted the need for progress but aesthetically he could not escape being a traditionalist. In this conundrum he was engaged in one of the key conflicts of his generation. There were those modernists who, like the Tecton group, espoused the Modern cause and built uncompromisingly modern-looking buildings. By contrast, there were those traditionalists who resorted to past styles to clothe their buildings: neo-Georgian, Tudorbethan and so on. North belonged to neither camp. He hated the flat-roof concrete-box aesthetic, but he also detested pastiche. In fact, he hated the idea of any style. He might have accepted being ascribed to the *Gothic* tradition, provided the emphasis was placed on the *spirit* of Gothic rather than the *aesthetic*. He said to a colleague: 'I don't feel that I'm a Gothic revivalist, I feel that I'm a reincarnation of the thirteenth century'.[59] This was something similar to what Lethaby had in mind when he wrote to Sydney Cockerell in 1915: 'As to Morris's Gothicism I think he saw modernness primarily as a principle, some places it is expressed quite clearly, and he used the word 'Gothic' in a special sense, not only historically for the fourth century on, but also for now and the future in the sense of people's art and the organic building art' (Lethaby 1915, in Rubens 1986: 153). In discussing Lethaby's Melsetter chapel (1900), Godfrey Rubens says it is 'not a Gothic Revival building, for no recognisable medieval form was employed. Yet – fresh, strong and savage – Gothic in Morris's sense it certainly is' (Rubens 1986: 153). This is exactly North's sort of Gothic, stripped down to the minimum so that, give or take a Gothic arch or two used sparingly over a fireplace or a front door, it almost becomes modern in its lean simplicity.

North must have been aware of the stylistic tightrope he was walking, especially when the pressure to design economically, particularly in the field of housing, was pushing architects away from the picturesque towards the cheaper, stripped-down classical style inspired by Georgian terraces. A few raw nerves of North's must have been touched when Weaver discussed this issue in 1926:

'I know there are still people who think that beauty lurks in barge boards and little oriel windows and the quirks and tricks of the pre-war speculative builder which can be catalogued as 'quaint', but their number is growing less. The attempt at prettiness has too long been the curse of architecture, the attempt to capture the elusive beauty of the craftsmanship of past centuries in our day, when the men and the social organism of which they were a part have passed into the limbo of history.

But the public taste has happily set steadily in a return to eighteenth-century traditions, and we have the right to be Georgian in our houses as in our loyalties. For the eighteenth century was the Age of Reason, and to that our architecture is returning.

With the Gothic Revival of the nineteenth century common sense departed. People wanted their houses served up like little abbeys on toast, and enthusiasts feared for their salvation if their kitchen windows lacked a pointed head.[1] (Weaver 1926: 2-3).

North persevered, but it may not be entirely coincidental that at his housing in Bangor, built a year after Weaver's book, there are no Gothic arches at all.

North may not have been a self-publicist like Baillie Scott, but his houses did find their way into contemporary building journals and Weaver's books. An article, which *The Builder* featured in 1918 when appraising entries for the RIBA/LGB housing competition, even hinted that among architectural circles North had some kind of national reputation: it referred to elevations that 'recall at once some of the delightful work carried out by Mr North in north Wales'. In 1968 John Betjeman, poet and sympathetic campaigner for British architecture, was to write in a letter to Frank Dann:

'If one could make a comparison, I would say that North is to Wales what Voysey, the early Lutyens and Baillie Scott were to England, and what George Walton and C. R. Mackintosh were to Glasgow and the lowlands of Scotland.'[60]

This accolade is praise indeed, representing North as a significant contributor to national style, but it should perhaps be seen in the context in which it was written when supporters were seeking to save St Winifred's chapel from demolition. A more realistic comparison should perhaps be made, not with the well-known national architects, but with the often very good regional architects throughout Britain, many of whom, like North, are yet to be recognised. John Coates Carter (1857-1927) in south Wales and Frank Hearn Shayler (1854-1954) in mid-Wales are cases in point.

North was a modest and self-effacing man. There is a story that he wanted all his drawings and records destroyed when he died.[61] If he was to be remembered, he would probably have preferred his church work to be his testimony rather than his houses, though it is the latter that so readily command admiration today. St Winifred's School chapel and his two new churches demonstrate an architectural competence and an ability to handle space and daylight in a way that his smaller-scale domestic work did not permit. Had he had the opportunity to build a church or two in north Wales, there is little doubt that these, combined with his record of domestic work, would have raised his reputation to one of real significance. It did not matter that architects elsewhere were straying down historicising paths (North might have said 'dead-ends') or were embracing the new forms of the Modern Movement. Herbert North kept to his own brand of modern Gothic, believing it was not a style as such but just the natural outcome of an honest, economic and appropriate way of building.

Two generations after Herbert North's death he is deeply admired by those who already know his buildings, and appreciation of his work is still growing. There is yet an opportunity for his influence to increase as architects, planners, owners and developers learn lessons from the way in which he lived out his principles of tradition, function and economy – ideas that readily translate into today's concerns with local distinctiveness, comfort and sustainability.

Notes and references

• INTRODUCTION

1 'Eventual' because his mother Fanny lived into her nineties and held onto the family wealth long after it might have passed to North.

• CHAPTER ONE

2 He was Honorary Secretary of the Leicestershire Architectural and Archaeological Society, a Fellow of the Society of Antiquaries and an established campanologist.

3 Letters in the archives of Pam Phillips (the spelling errors in the extracts are authentic).

4 Clough Williams-Ellis, too, had been moved at an early age to become a parson.

5 Probably an ordinary degree, consisting of a 'general' paper and a selection of 'special' subject papers; the degree course in architecture was not established until 1912.

6 North's scrapbooks contain a drawing of the cathedral, autographed by Bentley in 1895.

7 Welbeck Abbey chapel (Nottinghamshire), built 1890-96 and derived from Sedding's Our Holy Redeemer, Clerkenwell.

8 His brother, the Revd Arthur Tooth, had in 1877 been the first clergyman to be imprisoned for Ritualism.

9 Undated letter in the SPAB archives for Tintagel.

10 In a taped interview with Ian Allan in 1980, but Pam Phillips doubts this was true (see page 128).

11 His employment with Pite is listed in the RIBA Directory of British Architects 1834-1914.

12 Davies had remarried.

• CHAPTER TWO

13 Published in British Architect in May 1898. North designed further schemes for a new church at Caerhun and at an unidentified location in the Conwy valley, but none was ever built. Only the Church Hall at Caerhun came to fruition, in 1902 (see page 103).

14 See Davey 1995 and Cruickshank 1999.

15 R. Randal Phillips featured a large thatched house at Hythe by Oswald Milne for a Col. J. M. Graham (Phillips, 1925). Could this have been the same client?

16 Plas Llanfair, built 1863.

17 Originally called Rosebriers (an early drawing at the Royal Commission refers to the house as 'The Grove' but Pam Phillips says that the house was never known by this name).

18 Though not the front door, interestingly.

19 Undated cutting in one of North's early scrapbooks, probably 1899.

20 North had a copy of William Morris, his Art, his Writings and his Public Life: a Record by Aymer Vallance (1898 edition) in which Red House was published for the first time. In his scrapbooks are numerous photos of the house and its fittings.

• CHAPTER THREE

21 See Appendix 4 in Allan 1988, giving excerpts from Llanfairfechan UDC Minute Book 1904-08 (Gwynedd County Archives, Caernarfon Record Office, LXJ2/112/3).

22 The plan is very similar to Prior's butterfly-plan design for a cottage in Dorset, displayed at the Royal Academy in 1895.

23 Taped interview between Ian Allan and P. M. Padmore, April 1980.

24 Planned by Raymond Unwin in 1912 for the Cardiff Workers' Co-operative Garden Village Society Ltd; houses designed by A. H. Mottram, and a later phase by T. Alwyn Lloyd, who designed a number of estates in mid-Wales.

25 Taped interview between Ian Allan and P. M. Padmore, April 1980 (see page 128).

26 P. M. Padmore related this to Ian Allan (taped interview, 1980) (see page 128).

27 Talk on Herbert North, given in January 2009 at the Art Workers' Guild, London, as part of a Victorian Society study day on provincial architects.

28 The quarry he used most frequently was at Gallt-y-llan, near Nant Peris (taped interview of Frank Tyldesley, North's favourite builder, by Ian Allan, 1981) (see page 128).

29 Talfor and Gorsefield (1906) were built of brick to reduce loads on the concrete raft required because of the sandy seaside location.

30 Taped interview of Frank Tyldesley by Ian Allan, 1981 (see page 128).

31 Perhaps from Comyn Ching (in a taped interview, Tyldesley could not recall the supplier but remembered a double-barrel name).

32 Ironically, by the LGB President, Hayes Fisher.

33 The competition brief required the group of houses to include one end-of-terrace unit, one mid-terrace unit and one wide-frontage, single-room-deep unit. Consequently most entries had very similar block plans. See *Cottage Designs* (RIBA 1918) for full coverage of the competition brief and entries.

34 Hungarian-born Modernist architect (1902-1987), settled in London in 1934.

• CHAPTER FOUR

35 Many of these are in the North Collection (see List, page 127).

36 At this date, if it was a referral, it probably came through the League's predecessor, the Clergy & Artists Association.

37 St Cyngar, Borth-y-gest (Porthmadog).

38 He also designed a church tower for St Mary's, but it was not built.

39 Letter from North to the Revd Jones, dated 16 March 1934, now in the possession of Mr Harvey Lloyd.

40 See *The Architects' and Builders' Journal*, 7 September 1910, and the ICBS records of the West Shore church (ICBS 11043).

41 From *Merton Abbey Churches and Halls*, a brochure, dated 1925, in the archives of Pam Phillips.

42 For instance, 'Architectural Developments during Victoria's Reign' by F. M. Simpson (*Architectural Review*, 1897), 'Albi Cathedral' by H. Corlette (*Architectural Review*, 1900) and articles by James Cubitt in *The Building News*, 1869, republished in his book 'Church Designs for Congregations' (1870).

43 By Edward Maufe, Hubert Worthington, W J Palmer-Jones, A G Crimp and J Harold Gibbons (29 July, 1932).

44 The church is not identified in the book but it was designed in 1913 by Vivian H. King.

45 Information supplied by Andy Foster.

46 The commission was probably through Glyn Simon, who became Warden of St Michael's College in 1940 (and later Dean, then Bishop of Llandaff).

47 According to Padmore in a taped interview by Ian Allan, 1980.

48 His scrapbooks contain magazine photographs of some of them, surprisingly. For instance, a flat-roofed and very cubic church in Budapest by Bertalan Arkay looks a most unlikely candidate for North's attention until one notices that the plan must have reminded him of his plans for St Winifred's School chapel and his Guildford cathedral design.

49 For Hammond, the churches in this last category did not have to look modern architecturally - Ninian Comper's St Philip, Cosham (1938) was perfectly fitted to its purpose, regardless of its historicising style.

• CHAPTER FIVE

50 Taped interview of R. S. Nickson by Ian Allan, 1983.

51 Ibid.

52 The school pre-dates, by only a few years, the experimental 'open air' schools designed for the Caernarvonshire Education Committee by Rowland Lloyd Jones. These had large areas of south-facing windows which could be folded back to let in the fresh air. The 'open air' school movement was pioneered in Germany around 1904.

53 Taped interview of Frank Tyldesley by Ian Allan, 1981.

54 Interview of Gwen Thomas by Ian Allan, 1980 (see page 128).

55 The Woodard Corporation was founded in the mid-nineteenth century by Nathaniel Woodard, an Anglo-Catholic clergyman, who set up schools throughout Britain to cater for the education of the lower middle class. These now form the largest group of independent Church of England schools in the country. North designed buildings for a number of them in addition to St Winifred's: St Chad's, Denstone (Staffs); All Saints', Bloxham (Oxfordshire); St Oswald's, Ellesmere (Shropshire); and St Cuthbert's, Worksop (Notts). A classroom block survives at Denstone, but work at the other schools remains unrecorded or was not executed. His unbuilt scheme for Bloxham was vastly over-budget, despite following the clients' brief fastidiously - taped interview of Miss Margaret Heyworth by Ian Allan, 1981.

• CHAPTER SIX

56 Padmore's drawing of Highlands, Colwyn Bay, clearly shows where his straight-headed fireplace openings have been rubbed out by North and replaced with Gothic arches.

57 The title of an essay in *Form in Civilisation* (Lethaby 1924).

58 See footnote 41 to Chapter 5.

59 Taped interview of R. S. Nickson by Ian Allan, February 1983.

60 Letter from John Betjeman to Frank Dann, 5 September 1968.

61 Pam Phillips thinks this remark may have originated with her father, Padmore.

Key to Map

A Troutbeck Bridge
B Higher Bebington
C Llanddulas
D Colwyn Bay
E Llanfairfechan
F Bangor
G Dolgellau
H Brithdir
I Shrewsbury
J Harlescott
K Stafford
L Leicester
M Uppingham
N Cambridge
O London
P Oxford
Q Blackwell
R Cellan
S Llanybydder
T Tintagel
U Torquay

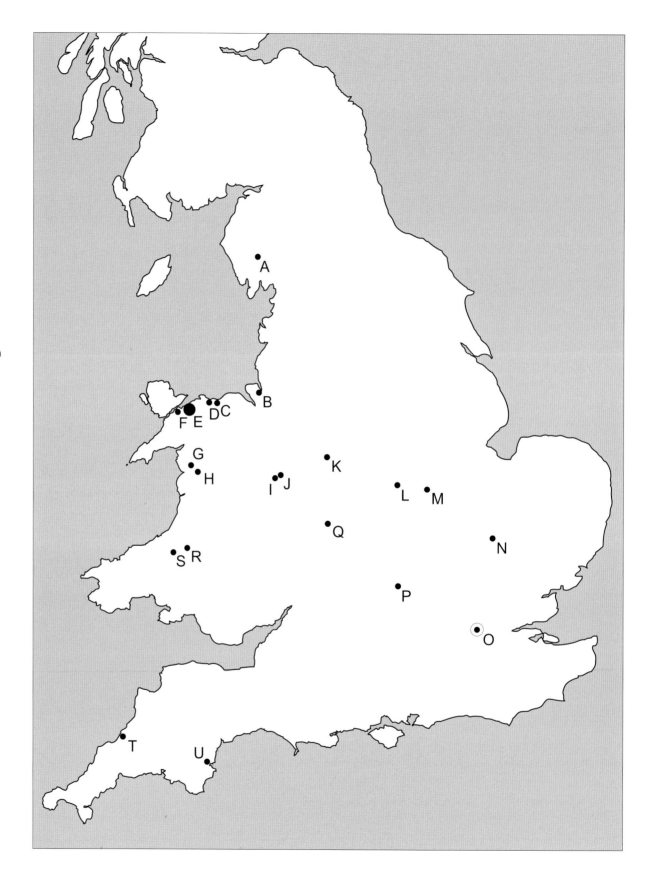

Chronological List of Selected Works

Italics denote unexecuted or demolished buildings.
The houses in The Close are numbered sequentially, not chronologically.

DATE	NAME	ADDRESS	NOTES	SOURCES OF INFORMATION
?	*Proposed design for a town church in red brick and granite*	–	–	NMRW
1898	*Proposed church at Caerhun*	–	–	NMRW
?	*Design for two country houses in thatch and roughcast*	–	–	NMRW
1898	Plas Llanfair Cottage	Village Road, Llanfairfechan	Additions to house designed by George Benmore for North's grandfather	–
1898	Bolnhurst	5 The Close, Llanfairfechan	–	Haslam 2009 Weaver 1913 Weaver 1926
1899	Northcot	Park Road, Llanfairfechan	North himself gives Northcot a later date than Bolnhurst though it looks earlier	Haslam 2009
1899	*Proposed lodge*	*Penrhiwardir, Tal-y-cafn*	*Possibly built in 1899, then altered in 1928; or the 1928 lodge was new (see later)*	*BJ Dec. 1899*
1899	*Builders' Journal competition*	–	*For a country house in Hythe. North came first but his design was not executed*	*NMRW BJ May 1899 BJ July 1899*
?	*Proposed mission church near Conwy*	–	–	NMRW
1900	Wern Isaf	Penmaen Park, Llanfairfechan	Formerly 'The Grove' and 'Rosebriers'; North's home/office; remarkably unaltered	Haslam 2009 NMRW Drury 2000
1902	Parish hall, Caerhun	B5106, Ty'n-y-groes, (Conwy)	Now a dwelling	Haslam 2009
1902	*Proposed church at Caerhun*	–	–	NMRW
1903-4	School	Henryd Road, Gyffin, Conwy	–	Haslam 2009 NMRW

DATE	NAME	ADDRESS	NOTES	SOURCES OF INFORMATION
1903	Ty'n Coed (formerly Woodcot)	6 The Close, Llanfairfechan	–	–
1903	Llangelynin (new) church	between Henryd & Ro-wen	–	Haslam 2009 NMRW
1904	Cefn Uchaf	Ro-wen (Conwy)	Alterations and additions to existing house	–
1904	Cefn Isaf	Ro-wen (Conwy)	New house, later extended by North (1908)	Haslam 2009 NMRW
1904	Proposed church	Harrowby Road, Grantham	–	NMRW
?	Proposed mission church	Conwy area	–	NMRW
1904	Design for reredos and canopy	–	'In a new church at Caerhun'	NMRW
1906	Talfor & Gorsefield	West Shore (The Cob), Llanfairfechan	Pair of semi-detached houses; Talfor altered internally and with new addition; Gorsefield hardly altered	Haslam 2009 Weaver 1913 H&G May 1920 H&G Jan. 1924
1906	'The Old Churches of Arllechwedd'	–	Book, published by Jarvis & Foster, Bangor	–
1907	Whilome	7 The Close, Llanfairfechan	Many internal and external features survive	–
1907	Lodge	Plas Heulog, Mount Road, Llanfairfechan	Formerly 'Newry'	Haslam 2009 NMRW
1908	Cellan church	Cellan, Lampeter, (Ceredigion)	Alterations to fabric, fittings and decorations	Lloyd 2006
1908	'The Old Cottages of Snowdonia'	–	Book, written with Harold Hughes	–
1908	Design for cottages at Conwy	–	Built in 1919	NMRW
1909	Design for a cottage at Deganwy	–	Notes added to the drawing, possibly by the disgruntled and dissatisfied client, suggest this project was abandoned	NMRW

DATE	NAME	ADDRESS	NOTES	SOURCES OF INFORMATION
1910	*Proposed church*	*St Saviour, Bryniau Road, West Shore, Llandudno*	*Competition entry, won by R. T. Beckett*	*NMRW*
1910	*Christ Church, Stafford*	*Demolished*	*Fittings and decorations*	*NMRW*
1910-11	Keldwith	Keldwith Drive, Troutbeck Bridge, Windermere, Westmorland	Large butterfly-plan house, now divided into three; mostly unchanged externally; some features survive internally. Gazebo added by North in 1913	Weaver 1922 Hyde 2010 Drury 2000 NMRW
1912	Church Institute	Park Road, Llanfairfechan	Remarkably unchanged	Haslam 2009 NMRW
1912	Cottages	Glan-y-mor Elias, Llanfairfechan	Pair of semi-detached cottages, little changed externally	–
1912	Beamsmoor	Park Road, Llanfairfechan	Largish house, fairly unaltered	NMRW
1912	Christ Church, Llanfairfechan	–	Fittings and decoration	Haslam 2009
1912	Northfield	1 The Close, Llanfairfechan	–	–
1913	Boathouse at Keldwith	On shore of Windermere	Wooden building	–
1913	Cottage at Keldwith	On lane above Troutbeck Bridge	Built for the chauffeur/gardener	–
1913	Llys-y-gwynt	Dolwyddelan, (Gwynedd)	Much altered	–
1913	Vicarage	Llanybydder, Lampeter, (Ceredigion)	Little altered	Lloyd 2006 NMRW
1913	*Country Life cottage competition*	–	*North's design was 'an individual conception', according to Weaver who was one of the assessors*	*Weaver 1913*
1915	*Proposed cottages*	*Abergwynant estate, Dolgellau*	–	*NMRW*

DATE	NAME	ADDRESS	NOTES	SOURCES OF INFORMATION
1918	LGB/RIBA Cottage competion	–	North won 1st premium in Class A, and 2nd in Classes C&D	The B Feb. 1918 BN Feb/Jun. 1918
1919	Houses	2 & 4 Bryn Hyfryd Park, Conwy	North did designs for these in 1908	Haslam 2009 NMRW
1920	Cwm Penmachno church	Cwm Penmachno, Betws-y-coed, (Gwynedd)	Conversion of school to church and hall; now a dwelling	Haslam 2009 NMRW
1920	Housing	–	20 semi-detached houses designed for Llanfairfechan UDC	NMRW
1921	Christ Church, Stafford	Demolished	Lady Chapel fittings and decorations	NMRW
1921	Christ Church, Llanfairfechan	–	Lady Chapel fittings and decorations	Haslam 2009
1922	Brooklands Coedfa The Haven	2 The Close 3 The Close 4 The Close	Little changed externally – –	– – –
1922	St Winifred's School, Llanfairfechan	Plas Gwyn, Station Road, Demolished	Temporary wooden chapel, hall and music wing	NMRW
1923	'Merton Abbey' buildings	–	'Designs for inexpensive churches and halls', for Morris & Co; the first chapel at St Winifred's School and the cottage at Wern Isaf were based on these designs	NMRW
1924	St Winifred's School	Demolished	Alterations at Plas Gwyn and laboratory	NMRW
1924	'The Old Churches of Snowdonia'	–	Book, written with Harold Hughes; nearly identical to North's 1906 book but expanded to include more churches	–
1925	Rose Lea Tŷ Hwnt yr Afon Hill Croft (formerly Llys Hywel) Maes Aled (formerly Cloud End) Parciau (formerly Westernie) Araulfan Carreg Fran (formerly Crowstones)	8 The Close 9 The Close 10 The Close 11 The Close 12 The Close 13 The Close 16 The Close	– – – – – – –	H&G Sep. 1926 – – H&G Jun. 1928 – – –
1925	Cottages	1-4 Bryn Haul, Bryn Road Llanfairfechan	Similar to the houses proposed for the UDC in 1920	–

DATE	NAME	ADDRESS	NOTES	SOURCES OF INFORMATION
1925	St Mary's, Llanfairfechan	Penybryn Road, Llanfairfechan	Screen, chancel skylight and other work	–
1925	Wern Isaf Bach	Penmaen Park, Llanfairfechan	Wooden cottage for the cook and chauffeur	–
1925	Monkswell Park	Ilsham, Marine Drive, Torquay (Devon)	Butterfly-plan house; much altered, particularly internally	Cherry 1989
1926	Churchmen's Club	Park Road, Llanfairfechan	Next door to the Church Institute	–
1926	Greenhills	24 The Close	–	–
	Neuadd Wen	25 The Close	–	Chatterton 1926
1926	*St Winifred's School*	*Park Road site Demolished*	*Classroom wing*	*NMRW*
1927	Sandy Lodge	28 Jack Straw's Lane, Headington, Oxford	Slightly different from the initial design	NMRW
1927	Housing	Seiriol Road, Bangor	20 terraced houses for COPEC; altered internally	Welsh Outlook
1928	Efrydfa	15 The Close	–	–
	Bryn Ffawydd	17 The Close	–	–
	Grey Gables	22 The Close	–	–
1928	Lodge	Penrhyd Cottage, Tal-y-cafn (Conwy)	Similar to the 1899 design, possibly a remodelling	–
1928-29	Dolgellau Hospital	Hospital Drive, Dolgellau	Extended by North in 1933 and 1938; further alterations and extensions (not by North)	–
1929-30	*St Winifred's School*	*Park Road site Demolished*	*Dean Roberts Hall, Ida North music wing, chapel*	*NMRW*
1930	House	30 Ffriddoedd Road, Bangor	–	–
1930	Guildford Cathedral competition	–	There was no winner and the competition seems to have been abandoned; in 1932, a short-list of architects was drawn up, and Edward Maufe's scheme was chosen	NMRW

DATE	NAME	ADDRESS	NOTES	SOURCES OF INFORMATION
1931	Swanston Cottage	1 Lever Causeway, Higher Bebington, Wirral, Merseyside	Most of the windows renewed, and the interior altered, but Vita glass in the loggia windows still in place (late 2010)	H&G Sept. 1931
1931	Trewen	14 The Close	–	H&G Aug. 1932
1933	*St Winifred's School*	*Park Road site Demolished*	*Sanatorium*	*A&BN Sept.1934 NMRW*
1933	Chaplaincy chapel	Church Hostel, Princes Road, Bangor	Altered; Alice Williams memorial library added by North in 1938	A&BN Aug.1935 NMRW
1933	Houses, Vardre Park	30, 32, 34, 36, 38, 54, 56, 58 Deganwy Road, Deganwy, Llandudno	Windows and interiors altered; Padmore designed the later houses	–
1933	Whitefriars	West Shore (The Cob), Llanfairfechan	Garage by Padmore (later)	NMRW
1935	Houses	4-6 Ael-y-bryn Road, Colwyn Bay	–	–
1935	Highlands (formerly Penwartha)	Hafodty Lane, Colwyn Bay	–	–
1935	Hafod (formerly Arsyllfa)	Tŷ Du Road, Llansanffraid, Glan Conwy	Butterfly-plan house; interior altered	–
1935	Hillcrest	21 The Close	–	–
1934-6	Harlescott Church	Church of the Holy Spirit, Roselyn, Harlescott, Shrewsbury	New church, with fittings; much altered and extended, now a social club	Anson 1965 Newman 2006 Thomas 2002 NMRW ICBS 1936 AD&C Feb. 1937 A&BN Aug.1936 A&BN Jan. 1937
1936	Ael-y-gwynt	18 The Close	–	A&BN Aug. 1936

DATE	NAME	ADDRESS	NOTES	SOURCES OF INFORMATION
1936	Tan-y-coed	School Lane, Llanfair Talhaearn, Abergele (Conwy)	Altered, but some internal features survive	–
1936	*Church design*	–	*For 'A Simple Suburban Church'*	*NMRW*
1937	Houses	Halfryn Tŷ Gwyn Wyniat Minffordd Road, Llanddulas (Conwy)	All altered and extended – –	– – –
1937	Dwyfor	23 The Close	–	–
1938	Llangernyw Church	St Digain, Llangernyw, Abergele (Conwy)	Screen	–
1939	Bryn-y-mor	Llys Helyg Drive, West Shore, Llandudno	For Frank Tyldesley, North's favourite builder, to whom he gave the plans as a wedding present	–
1939-41	Blackwell Church	St Catherine, The Linthurst, Blackwell, Bromsgrove, (Worcs)	New church, with fittings etc; completed in 1941, after North's death	Brooks 2007 NMRW A&BN Mar.1941
1939	*Design for a chapel*	–	*For St Michael's College, Llandaff*	*NMRW*
1940	Acorn Cottage	19 The Close	Much extended	A&BN Nov. 1940
1940	RIBA Industrial Housing competition	–	–	JRIBA Sep.1940 JRIBA July 1940
?	Unidentified church designs	–	–	NMRW

"The Close" Building Estate,

Llanfairfechan,
North Wales.

LLANFAIRFECHAN, situated between the Mountains and the Sea, occupies one of the most beautiful positions in Snowdonia.

The Climate is very Sunny and Dry, and the hills sheltering it from the North and East make it an ideal Winter Resort. It is also very accessible from Liverpool, Manchester and the Midlands, being on the main Chester to Holyhead rail and road.

The Estate, though close to the Village, is situated in the midst of beautiful well wooded park land, with most lovely unspoilt views of Mountain and Sea.

The Houses, which are of picturesque design and sound construction, with town water, main drainage and gas, are labour saving in plan and fittings, and each one is built to suit the requirements of the Purchaser at very reasonable cost; also the Sites are very moderate in price and are free from all charges.

For further particulars apply to the owner, Mr. H. L. North, Llanfairfechan.

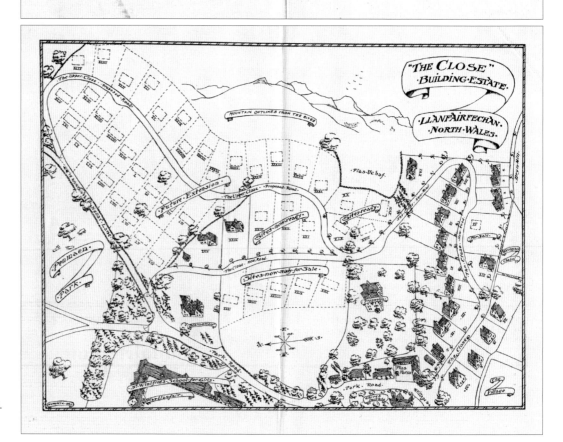

North's prospectus for The Close.

Herbert Luck North Collection

*Items are listed with the National Monuments Record of Wales catalogue number and the
National Primary Record Number (NPRN), which are used on the public online database www.coflein.gov.uk.*

NAME OF BUILDING	NPRN	CATALOGUE Nos	
DOMESTIC			
Abergwynant, cottages at	–	13861	Drawing
Acorn Cottage, Llanfairfechan	96649	13860	Drawing
Beamsmoor, Llanfairfechan	470	13256, 17487	Photographs
Cefn Isaf, Ro-wen	472	13259	Photographs of house before extension
Conwy, Brynhyfryd Cottages	96650	13871	Drawing
Cottages, 4	–	13857	Drawing
Cottages for Llanfairfechan U.D.C.	–	13859	Drawing
Cottages, vernacular	–	13851, 17423, 17456	Drawings
Country house near Hythe (competition)	–	13198, 13200, 13220, 13221	Coloured drawings
Country house, 2 sketches for a	–	13206	Drawings
Deganwy, cottage at		13872	Drawing
Houses, unidentified	–	13205, 13212	Drawings
House in The Close for Lord Olivier	–	13861	Drawing
Industrial housing competition (1940)	–	13211	Drawing
Keldwith, Windermere	–	13216-18, 13228-13234, 13244, 13264-6	Good set of working drawings, photographs
ditto (early design)	–	13235	Drawing
Llŷn Traffwll, cottage at	96656	13876	Drawing
Newry, lodge at	96663, 469	13213, 13849, 17425, 17451	Working drawings
Oxford, house at Headington	–	13194	Drawing
Oxford, White Gables	–	13245-6	Drawings
Shenstone, cottage near	–	13237	Drawing
Tal-y-cafn, lodge at	96657	13877, 17437-9, 17436, 17441-6	Working drawings
Trearddur Bay, house at	–	13875	Drawing
Wern Isaf, Llanfairfechan	301624	17433, 17437-9, 17452	Working drawings
CHURCH WORK			
Bangor, Chaplaincy chapel	25997	13253-4, 17488	Photographs
Blackwell, St Catherine	–	13195-7, 13227, 13243, 17485	Drawings, photographs
Caerhun (1898 design)	–	13858	Drawing
Caerhun (1902 design)	–	17467	Drawing

NAME OF BUILDING	NPRN	CATALOGUE Nos.	
Caerhun (design for a reredos)	–	13856	Coloured drawing
Cwm Penmachno	–	13862	Drawing
Grantham	–	13219	Coloured drawing
Guildford Cathedral (competition)	–	13222-6	Drawings
Harlescott, Holy Spirit	–	13248-52, 13260-3, 17486	Drawings, photographs
Llanbadoc Fawr, St Madoc (screen)	96655	13867	Coloured Drawing
Llandudno, West Shore	–	17416, 17426	Drawings
Llangelynin (old church)	–	17466	Drawing
Llangelynin (new church)	–	13869-70, 17454	Coloured drawings
Merton Abbey church halls	–	13240-1	Drawings
Mission church, design for a	–	13868	Drawing
Newtown, St Mary	96660	17428, 17430-2	Drawings
Porth, St Paul	96652	13863	Drawing
Simple Suburban Church, A	–	13202	Drawing
Stafford, Christ Church	–	13242	Coloured drawing
Town churches, design for two	–	13203, 13204	Coloured drawings
Unidentified churches	–	13201, 13208-10	Drawings
Various (north Wales churches)	–	13855	Drawings
Church fittings	–	13214-5, 13236, 13238-9, 17429, 17470-84	Drawings

OTHER BUILDINGS

Bryncoedifor school	–	13864	Drawing
Church Institute, Llanfairfechan	471	13257-8, 17489	Photographs
Gyffin school	96659	13199, 17419, 17434-5, 17447-50	Good set of working drawings
Llandaff, St Michael's College chapel	–	13841, 13854	Drawings
Llanybydder vicarage	–	13866	Drawings
St Winifred's School, Llanfairfechan	–	13267, 13848, 17417-8, 17422, 17440, 17455	Drawings, photographs

TAPES OF INTERVIEWS BY IAN ALLAN

With P. M. Padmore, 24th April 1980	411464	
With Mr and Mrs Padmore (Mary Allan also present), 24th April and 29th May 1980	411464	
With Frank Tyldesley (Vernon Hughes also present), 26th May 1981	411464	
With Miss Margaret Heyworth, 21st September 1981	411464	
With R. S. Nickson (Peter Howell also present), 12th February 1983	411464	

Bibliography

Marked * where there is a specific reference to North's buildings.

Allan, I.B. 1979 & 1980. Henry Wilson's Brithdir Letters, Parts 1 & 2, *Journal of the Merioneth Historical and Record Society.*

Allan, I.B. 1988. *The Life and Work of H. L. North.* Unpublished PhD thesis, University of Liverpool.*

Anson, P. 1965. *Fashions in Church Furnishings.* London: Studio Vista.*

The Architect and Building News [Guildford Cathedral competition] 12 December 1930, 781.

The Architect and Building News [Guildford Cathedral competition] 29 July 1932, 122-140.

The Architect and Building News [St Winifred's] 28 Sept 1934, Vol. CXXXIX, 380-1.*

The Architect and Building News [Chaplaincy chapel] 16 August 1935, Vol. CXLIII, 198.*

The Architect and Building News [Ael-y-gwynt] 14 August 1936, Vol. CXLVII, 199.*

The Architect and Building News [Harlescott church] 8 January 1937, Vol. CXLIX, 42-3.*

The Architect and Building News [Acorn Cottage] 8 November 1940, Vol. CLXIV, 90.*

The Architect and Building News [Blackwell church] 14 March 1941, Vol. CLXV, 177-8.*

Architectural Design and Construction [Harlescott church] February 1937, Vol. VII, 153.*

Baillie Scott, M. H. 1906. *Houses and Gardens.* London: George Newnes Ltd.

The British Architect [perspective of Caerhun church design] 6 May 1898.*

Brooks, A. and Pevsner, N. 2007. *The Buildings of England: Worcestershire.* London: Yale University Press.*

The Builder. Local Government Board and RIBA Cottage Competition. January-June 1918, 123.*

The Builders' Journal [Hythe house competition, brief] 3 May 1899, 186.*

The Builders' Journal [Hythe house competition, results] 5 July 1899, 321-3.*

The Builders' Journal [new lodge at Tal-y-cafn] 27 December 1899.*

The Building News [LGB/RIBA Cottage Competition] 20 February 1918, 140-141.*

The Building News [LGB/RIBA Cottage Competition] 26 June 1918, 449.*

Chatterton, F. (ed.) 1926. *Houses Cottages and Bungalows.* London: Architectural Press.*

Cherry, B. and Pevsner, N. 1989. *The Buildings of England: Devon*, London: Penguin.*

Cruickshank, D. 1999. Material Values, *The Architects' Journal*, 18 November 1999, 34-49.

Davey, P. 1995. *Arts and Crafts Architecture.* London: Phaidon.

Dearmer, P. 1921. *The Parson's Handbook* (10th ed). Oxford: Humphrey Milford (first published in 1899).

Drury, M. 2000. *Wandering Architects.* Stamford: Shaun Tyas.*

Edwards, G. E. 1928. A North Wales Housing Experiment, *The Welsh Outlook*, Vol. XV.*

Haigh, D. 1995. *Baillie Scott: The Artistic House.* London: Academy Editions.

Hammond, P. 1960. *Liturgy and Architecture.* London: Barrie & Rockliff.

Haslam, R. 1996. *Clough Williams-Ellis* (RIBA Drawings Monographs No 2). London: Academy Editions.

Haslam, R., Orbach, J. and Voelcker, A. 2009. *The Buildings of Wales: Gwynedd,* London: Yale University Press.*

Hilling, J. 1975. *Plans & Prospects: Architecture in Wales 1780-1914* (Exhibition catalogue). Cardiff: Welsh Arts Council.*

Hilling, J. 1976. *The Historic Architecture of Wales.* Cardiff: University of Wales Press.*

Homes & Gardens [Talfor and Gorsefield] May 1920, Vol.1, 365.*

Homes & Gardens [ditto] January 1924, Vol.5, 274.*

Homes & Gardens [Roselea] September 1926, Vol.8, 135-6.*

Homes & Gardens [Cloud End] June 1928, Vol.10, 24.*

Homes & Gardens Three Houses of Today [house at Higher Bebington] September 1931, Vol.13, 161-2.*

Homes & Gardens [Trewen] August 1932, Vol.14, 118.*

Hubbard, E. 1986. *The Buildings of Wales: Clwyd.* London and Cardiff: Penguin.*

Hughes, H. and North, H. L. 1908. *The Old Cottages of Snowdonia.* Bangor: Jarvis & Foster (reprinted by the Snowdonia National Park Society, 1979).

Hughes, H. and North, H. L. 1924. *The Old Churches of Snowdonia.* Bangor: Jarvis & Foster (reprinted by the Snowdonia National Park Society, 1984).

Hyde, M. and Pevsner, N. 2010. *The Buildings of England: Cumberland and Westmorland*. London: Yale University Press.*

ICBS 1936. *New Churches Illustrated*. London: Incorporated Church Building Society.*

ICBS 1947. *Fifty Modern Churches*. London: Incorporated Church Building Society.

Kirk, K. E. 1937. *The Story of the Woodard Schools*. London: Hodder & Stoughton.*

Lethaby, W. R. 1891. *Architecture, Mysticism and Myth*. London: Percival & Co.

Lethaby, W. R. 1910. *R.I.B.A. Journal*, April, 476-9.

Lethaby, W. R. 1911. *Architecture*. London: Williams & Norgate.

Lethaby, W. R. 1924. *Form in Civilisation*. Reprinted by Oxford University Press, 1957.

Lloyd, T., Orbach, J., and Scourfield, R. 2006. *The Buildings of Wales: Carmarthenshire and Ceredigion*, London and Cardiff: Penguin.*

MacCarthy, F. 1994. *William Morris – A Life of Our Time*. London: Faber & Faber.

Newman, J. and Pevsner, N. 2006. *The Buildings of England: Shropshire*. London: Penguin.*

Nicholson, C. & Spooner, C. (n.d.) *Recent English Ecclesiastical Architecture*. London: Technical Journals Ltd. (probable date *c*.1911).

North, H. L. 1906. *The Old Churches of Arllechwedd*. Bangor: Jarvis & Foster.

Phillips, R. Randal 1925. *Small Country Houses of To-day (Vol.3)*. London: Country Life.

Powers, A. 2007. *Britain*. London: Reaktion Books.

R.I.B.A. 1918. *Cottage Designs*. London: RIBA.*

R.I.B.A. *Journal* [Industrial Housing Competition], 15 July 1940, 211.

R.I.B.A. *Journal* [Industrial Housing Competition], 19 August 1940, 244.

R.I.B.A. *Journal* [Industrial Housing Competition], 16 September 1940, 245-6

Roberts, N. (ed.) 1937. *St Winifred's, Llanfairfechan: The Story of Fifty Years*. Shrewsbury: Wilding & Son.*

Rubens, G. 1986. *William Richard Lethaby*. London: Architectural Press.

Scott, G. G. 1953. interview in *R.I.B.A. Journal*, April 1953, 224.

Swenarton, M. 1981. *Homes fit for Heroes*. London: Heinemann.

Thomas, J. 2002. *Albi Cathedral and British Church Architecture*. London: The Ecclesiological Society.*

Voysey, C. F. A. 1911. The English House, *The British Architect*, Vol. LXXV, 69.

Weaver, L. 1913. *The Country Life Book of Cottages*. London: Country Life.*

Weaver, L. 1922. *Small Country Houses of Today* (vol.2). London: Country Life.*

Weaver, L. 1926. *Cottages: their planning, design and materials*. London: Country Life.*

Wiliam, E. 2010. *The Welsh Cottage*. Aberystwyth: RCAHMW.

Williams-Ellis, C. 1991. *Architect Errant*. Portmeirion: Portmeirion Ltd (first published in 1971 by Constable & Co Ltd).

Index

Italic page numbers refer to illustrations and material in illustration captions.

Aberystwyth church 76
Acorn Cottage, The Close 125, 127
Ael-y-gwynt, The Close *56, 59, 60, 62*
Albi cathedral 83
All Saints, Brockhampton *88,* 89, 93, *94,* 100
All Saints, Cellan 75, *75*
Allan, Ian 7, 76, 107, 128
Allan, Mary 7
Araulfan, The Close 122
Arllechwedd, The Old Churches of 41, 101, 120
army service 67
Arsyllfa, Glan Conwy *see* Hafod
Art Workers' Guild 9
Arts & Crafts movement 9, 10, 16-17, 22, 27, 36,
    41, 50, 63, 66, 87, 105
Ashbee, Charles R. 9
Ayrton, O. M. 22

Baillie Scott, M. H. 9, 27, 36-7, *37,* 39, 42-3,
    106, 115
Bangor 40, 70-2, *70, 71,* 114, 115, 123;
    see also COPEC
    Church Hostel chapel 89-91
    St Peter's Church, Penrhosgarnedd *110,* 111
Barmouth 15
Barn, The, Exmouth 27, *35,* 36, *36*
Barnsley, Ernest 17
beams *63,* 63-4
Beamsmoor, Llanfairfechan 42, *62,* 66, 121, 127
Beckett, R. T. 79, 121
Beddgelert church 79
Benllech church 111
Benmore, George 29, *29,* 119
Bentley, John Francis 15
Betjeman, John 115

Betws-y-coed church 15
Blackwell church, Worcs 94-6, *94-6,* 112, 114,
    125, 127
Blow, Detmar 9, 17, 20, 27, *35,* 36, *36*
Bodley & Garner 83
Böhm, Dominikus 94
Bolnhurst, The Close 27, 29, *29, 30,* 31, 63, 66,
    94, 119
Bolton, Arthur 50
Bowen, Stewart Powell 112
Bowen Dann Davies 112
Brithdir church 9, *17,* 18, 19, *19,* 25
Broadleys, Windermere 50
Brockhampton church *88,* 89, 93, *94,* 100
Brooklands, The Close *58,* 122
Brooks, Alan 96
Brooks, James 15
Bryn Ffawydd, The Close 123
Bryn Haul, Llanfairfechan 70, 122
Bryn-y-mor, Llandudno 125
Bryncoedifor school 128
Bulkeley estate 13
Butterfield, William 15, 76
butterfly-plan 27, *31,* 36, *36, 47, 47,* 50, 50-1, *105,*
    123, 124

Caerdeon church 25-6, 25
Caerhun church *24,* 25, *77,* 78, *78,* 101, 119, 127-8
    church hall 103, *103* 119
Cambridge *37*
    Jesus College 15
Capel Curig church 77
Cardiff 53, *57*
    Workers' Co-operative Garden Village Society 116
    n.24
Caröe, W. D. 79
Carreg Fran, The Close 122
Carter, John Coates 115

Cefn Isaf, Ro-wen *41*, 43-5, *43-6*, 63, *63, 64, 65*, 120, 127

Cefnbuarddau, Llanaelhaearn 39

ceiling beams *63*, 63-4

Cellan church, Lampeter 75, 120

Charterhouse School chapel 84, *84*

Chesters, Northumberland 27, *36*

chimneys 60, *60*, 61

Christ Church, Llanfairfechan 13, 14, 76, 121, 122

Christ Church, Stafford 76, *77*, 121, 122, 128

Christian Order in Politics, Economics and Citizenship *see* COPEC

Church Crafts League 22, 75, 99

church halls 10, 79

Church Hostel chapel, Bangor 89-91, *89-91*, 124, 127

Church Institute, Llanfairfechan *59, 60*, 66, 104-5, *105*, 121, 128

Church of our Holy Redeemer, Clerkenwell 16

Church of the Holy Spirit, Harlescott *74*, 91-4, *92-3*, 101, 124

church pageants 10

church schools 10

churches 10, 14-17, *24*, 25-6, 41, 75-102
    interiors 75-7, 81, 83
    North's passion for 10, 14-16
    Snowdonian 21, 79, *98*, 101, 112

Churchmen's Club, Llanfairfechan 66, 106, *106*, 123

Close, The, Llanfairfechan *6-7*, 10, 13, 27-29, *30*, 31, 39, 40, 41-2, 51-7, *51-7, 58, 59, 60, 61, 62*, 63, 66, 94, 112, 119-25; aerial views 53; plan 52; prospectus 126

Cloud End, The Close 122

Cockerell, Sydney 114

Coedfa, The Close 122

Cogswell, W. G. St J. 22

Colwyn Bay 57, 124

Comper, Ninian 76, 87, 101

competitions *24*, 27, 36, 37, 40, 43, 50, 67-70, *67*, 72-3, *72-3*, 78-9, *86*, 87-9, 114, 119, 121-3, 125

concrete 114

Congres Internationaux d'Architecture Moderne (CIAM) 113

Conwy *58*, 75, 76, 120, 122, 125
    mission church design 78, *79*, 119
    valley 25, 39, 41, 50-1

COPEC Housing Group, Bangor 40, 70-2, *70, 71*, 123

Cordeliers church 83

cottage hospital 10, 107

cottages *37*, 38, 41, 50, 63, 112, 127
    Snowdonian *8, 40*, 41, 58, 59, 120
    labourers' *11*, 67, 68-9

country houses 26-7, *26*, 31, 37, 50, 119, 127

Cricklewood 22

Crossways 37

cupboards 33, *64*, 65, 67

Curtis Green, W. 94

Cwm Penmachno, Conwy 75, 122, 128

Dann, Frank 112, 115

Davies, Bill 112

Davies, J. B. (North's father-in-law) 14-15, 16, 22

Deanery Garden 22

Dearmer, Revd Percy 75, 94, 99

Deganwy 40, *57, 58, 60*, 120, 127

Dolgellau and Barmouth District Cottage Hospital 107, *107*, 123

doors 19, *34, 45*, 50, *62*, 63, *63*, 64-5, *64*

dormer windows 59-60, *60*

Douglas, John 81

Dudley Report 114

Durst, A. 20

Dwyfor, The Close *55, 61*, 125

Eden, F. C. 22, *91*, 101

Efrydfa, The Close 123

Ellis, Revd Philip Constable 14

embroideries 33, 76, 81

environment, concern for 11, 41, 115

Ewhurst 36

Exmouth, The Barn 27, *35*, 36, *36*

fireplaces 49, *49*, 50, 66, *66*

First World War 67, *68*

Foulkes, Sidney Colwyn 10-11

front doors *34, 45*, 50, *62*, 63, *63*

gables 31, 47, 58

galleries 29, 31

Gallt-y-llan quarry 116 *n.28*

garden villages 40, 53-7, 57, 69, 116 *n.24*

gardens 33-5, *43*, 45
    boundaries 51

Ghent Dominican church 83

Gibberd, Frederick 72

Gimson, Ernest 9, 17, 27, *35*, 36, *36*

Goddards 22

Goldfinger, Ernö 72

Gorsefield, Llanfairfechan 42, *42*, 116 *n.29*, 120

Gothic style 37, 47, 50, *62*, 63, 89, 94, 99, 100, 101, 105, 109, 114, 115

Graham, Col. J. M. 116 *n.15*

Greenhills, The Close 123

Grey, Edward 96

Grey Gables, The Close 63, 123

Grove, Arthur 17, 19-20

Grove, The *see* Wern Isaf

Guildford cathedral *86*, 87-9, *89*, 101, 114, 123, 128

Gyffin
    church 101
    school 103-4, *104*, 128

Hafod, Glan Conwy *50*, 51, *51*, 124

Halfryn, Llanddulas 125

halls *33, 37, 44, 49*

Hancocks, Buckley (bricks) 66

Happisburgh Manor 27, 36, *36*

Harlescott church, Shrewsbury *74*, 91-4, *92-3*, 101, 124, 128

Haslam, Richard 11

Haven, The Close 122

Headington, Oxford 39, 112, 123, 127

Hebert, Father Gabriel 101

Heyworth, Margaret 128

Higher Bebington, Wirral 50, 112, 124

Hill Croft, The Close 122

Hillcrest, The Close 124

Holy Spirit, Church of the, Harlescott *74*, 91-4, *92-3*, 101, 128

Holy Trinity, Bothenhampton 94,

Holy Trinity, Sloane Street 16, *16*

Home Place, Norfolk 27, *36*

Homewood 22

Hope, Henry & Sons 63

hospitals 10, 107

'house-place' *see also* halls 37

houses 26-37, 39-73, 112
    butterfly-plan *27, 31*, 36, *36*, 47, *47*, *50*, 50-1, *105*, 123, 124
    designs 24, 26-7, *26, 27*, 58-66
    private 41-57

housing
    industrial 72-3, *72-3*, 114
    private 41-57
    public 40, 67-73, 114
    standards 11, 68, 70
    workers' 11, 72-3, *72-3*

Hughes, Harold 76

Hughes, Vernon 7

Humphreys, G. A. 10, *11*, 21

Hythe competition *24, 27*, 36, 37, 43, 127

Incorporated Church Building Society 94, 101, 111

industrial housing 72-3, *72-3*, 114

internal buttress 83

Jekyll, Gertrude 22

Jesus College, Cambridge 15

Jones, R. Arthur 57

Keldwith, Lake District 27, 39, 41, 45, 47, 49-50, *47-9*, 64, 66, 112, 121, 127

Kempley church, Gloucs 81, *81*

Kennedy, Henry 29

Lake District 27, 37, *37*, 39, 41, 45-50, 112

Lee, J. S. 22

Lethaby, William 9, 35, *88*, 89, 93, 94, *94*, 100, 114

Liturgical Movement 99-100

Liverpool cathedral 84

Llanaelhaearn 39

Llanbadoc Fawr, Gwent 75

Llandaff, St Michael's College 96, *97*, 125, 128

Llanddulas 57

Llandudno 10, 78-81, *79*, 101

Llanfairfechan 9, 13, 27, 31, 39, 40, 42-3, *61, 62*, 63, 64, 66, *102*, 103, 104, 109, 116 *n.29*;
    see also Close, The
    Church Institute *59, 60*, 66, 104-5, *105*, 121, 128
    churches 13, 14, 76, 77, 121, 123
    Churchmen's Club 66, 106, *106*, 123
    Penmaen Park 31, *see also* Wern Isaf

St Winifred's school & chapel *80*, 82-7, *82, 84-5,*
    107-9,*108-9*
    Urban District Council 40, 69-70, *69*, 122, 127
Llangelynin church, Conwy *76*, 120, 128
Llangernyw church 125
Llanybydder vicarage 128
Lloyd, Harvey 7
Lloyd, T. Alwyn 116 *n.24*
Llys Hywel, The Close 122
Llys-y-gwynt 121
Local Government Board competition 67, 68
lodges 27, *28, 60, 61, 102*, 104, 127
Long Copse, Ewhurst 36
Luck
    Anne (North's grandmother) 13
    Richard (North's grandfather) 13, 22, 29, 33
Lutyens, Edwin Landseer 9, *21*, 22, 27, 50, 58, 115
Lytton, Lady Emily 22

Mackintosh, C. R. 115
Maes Aled, The Close 122
Marchant, Robert 22
Marsh Court 22
masonry 19
Maufe, Edward 89, *89*
Melsetter chapel 114
memorials *58*
Menai Strait 31
'Merton Abbey' buildings 81-2, *81*, 109, 114, 122, 128
Milne, Oswald 116 *n.15*
Minimum Dwelling 113-4
Modern Movement 101, 114, 115
Monkswell Park *see* Torquay
Moorcrag, Lake District 37
Morris, William 14, 17, 20, 31, 41, 75-6, 114
    textiles 75, 76, 81, 82, 87
Morris & Co. 81, 122 *see also* 'Merton Abbey' buildings
Mostyn estate 10
Mottram, A. H. 116 *n.24*
Munstead Wood 22

Neuadd Wen, The Close *6-7*, 123
Newry, Llanfairfechan *61, 102*, 104, 120, 127
Newton, Ernest 9
Nicholson, Charles 17, 101

Nickson, R.S. 103, 111, 128
North
    Fanny (Herbert's mother née Luck) 22, 103, 104
    Ida Joan (Herbert's daughter) 22, 111
    Ida Maude (Herbert's wife née Davies) 22, 23,
        76-7, *82*
    Thomas (Herbert's father) 13, 14, 22
Northcot, Llanfairfechan 27-29, *29*, 63, *66*, 119
Northfield, The Close 42, 121
Norton, R. 27
Norwich Town Hall 114

Old Post Office, Tintagel 9
Orchards, The 22
Overstrand Hall 22
Oxford 39, 112, 123, 127

Pace, George 96
Padmore, Perceval Mitchell 7, 9, 22, 53, 75, 111, 128
Pant Glas Uchaf *63*
Papillon Hall 27
Parciau, The Close *60*, 122
Parish Communion movement 101
passage aisle 83, 88
Pearson, J. L. 15, *15*, 83
Penmaen Park 31, *see also* Wern Isaf
Penmaenmawr 84
Pennant, Hon. Eleanor Douglas 108
Penrhiwardir, Flints. 27, 28, 119
Penrhosgarnedd, *see* Bangor
Penrhyn estate 29
Peterborough Cathedral 15
Petit, Revd. J. L. 25, *25*
Phillips, Pamela J. 7, 108
Phillips, R. Randal 116 *n.15*
Pinkerton, Godfrey 84
Pite, Beresford 22
Pite, W A. 22
Plas estate 31
Plas Gwyn, Llanfairfechan 108, 109
Plas Heulog *see* Newry, Llanfairfechan
Plas Llanfair, Llanfairfechan 13, 29, *29*, 33, 82, 108, 119
Platt, John 13
Plymouth, Earl of 96
porches 31, 58, *62*, 63

porte-cochère 47, *48*, 50

Powell, Alfred 17, 27, 36

Prior, Edward S. 9, 17, 27, 36, *36*, 50, *88*, 89, 93, 94, 100, 116 *n.22*

prisms *34*, 35, 45, 63

private housing 41-57

public housing 40, 67-73
    competitions 40, 67-70, 114

Quennell, Charles 17, 19-20

Rea, Alec 45

Red Cross service 67

Red House
    Bexleyheath 31, 33
    Douglas *37*

Rhiwbina garden village 53, *57*

Roker church *88*, 89, 93, 94, 100

roofs 11, 31, 47, 58-60
    chimneys 60, *60*, 61

room planning 67

Rose Court 37

Rose Lea, The Close 122

Rosebriers *see* Wern Isaf

Ro-wen *41*, 43, 63, *63*,

Royal Institute of British Architects (RIBA) 67, 67, 72, *72*, 114

Rubens, Godfrey 114

Ruskin, John 9, 17, 50

St Andrew, Plaistow 15

St Andrew, Roker *88*, 89, 93, 94, 100

St Apollinaris, Freilingsdorf 94

St Augustine, Kilburn 83

St Augustine, Pendlebury 83, *83*

St Catherine, Blackwell 94-6, *94-6*, 112, 114, 125, 127

St Celynin, Llangelynin *75*

St Chad, Bolton 111

St Christopher, Cove 94

St Clement, Bournemouth 17

St Cyngar, Borth-y-gest 116 *n.37*

St Edward the Confessor, Kempley 81, *81*

St George, Waddon 94

St John, Barmouth 15

St John, Kennington 15

St John the Evangelist, Holborn 15, *15*

St Madoc, Llanbadoc Fawr 75, 128

St Mark, Brithdir 9, *17*, *18*, 19, *19*, 25

St Mary, Aberystwyth 76

St Mary, Betws-y-coed 15

St Mary, Beverley 15

St Mary, Llanfairfechan 76, *77*, 123

St Mary, Newtown 128

St Mary, Summerstown 84

St Mary and All Saints, Conwy 76

St Michael's College, Llandaff 96, *97*, 125, 128

St Paul, Porth 128

St Peter, Barton-on-Humber 93

St Peter, Ealing 16

St Peter, Penrhosgarnedd, Bangor *110*, 111

St Philip, Caerdeon 25, *25*

St Saviour, West Shore, Llandudno 78-81, *79*, 101, 121, 128

St Winifred's School & chapel 57, *80*, 81, 82-7, *82*, *84-5*, 107-9, *108-9*, 115, 122, 123, 124, 128

Sts Andrew & Bartholomew, Ashleworth 75

Sandy Lodge, Headington 39, 112, 123, 127

Scott, George Gilbert 15, 84, *84*

Second World War 72, 73, 114

Sedding, John Dando 9, 15, 16, 17, 99

Seiriol Road, Bangor 70-2, *70*, *71*, 114, 115, 123

Shayler, Frank Hearne 115

Shaw, Richard Norman 9, 15, 27, 36

Shenstone, Staffordshire 112, 127

Shrewsbury *74*

shutters, window 65, *65*

Sikkel, Mary 7

Simon, Revd Glyn 91, 117

Simpson, J. W. 22

Snowdonia 22, 58
    'Country House in' competition 37
    house *63*
    Old Churches of 21, 79, 98, 101, 122
    Old Cottages of 8, 21, *37*, *40*, 41, 58, 59, 120

social housing 40, 67-72

Society for the Protection of Ancient Buildings (SPAB) 9, 20, 21, 76

spyholes *see* prisms

staircases 9, 65

Stoneywell Cottage, Ulverscroft 35, 36

Storey's Way 48, Cambridge *7*
Street, G. E. 15, 17
Swanston Cottage 124
Swenarton, Mark 68

Talfor, Llanfairfechan 42, *42*, 116 *n.29*, 120
Tal-y-cafn, Flints. 27, *28*, 50, 119, 123, 127
Tan-y-coed, Llanfair Talhaearn *66*, 125
Tecton 114
Thomas, Phil 7
Tigbourne Court 22
Tintagel, Old Post Office 9, 20, *20*
Tooth, Louisa 19
Tooth, Revd Charles 19
Torquay 39, 41, 50, 123
Trewen, The Close *57*, 124
Tudor Walters committee 68
Turner, Thackeray 20
Tŷ Gwyn, Llanddulas 125
Tŷ Hwnt yr Afon, The Close 122
Tyldesley, Frank 67, 106, 116 *n.28*, 128

Ulverscroft *35*, 36
Unwin, Raymond 68, 116 *n.24*
Uppingham School 7, 13

Vardre Park, Deganwy 57, *58, 60*, 124
vernacular, North's interest in *39*, 41, 112
Vita glass 114, 124
Voysey, Charles F. A. 9, 27, 37, 36-7, *37*, 50, 58, 63, 65, 115

walls 61, 114, 116 *n.29*
Walton, George 115
war service 67
Ward, W.H. 22
war-time housing 72-3
'We are Seven' memorial, Conwy *58*
Weaver, Lawrence 50, 104
Webb, Philip 9, 15-16, 31, 33
Weir, William 20-21
Welbeck Abbey chapel 16
Wells, A. Randall 81
Wern Isaf 9, 31-5, *31-5*, 36, 37, 41, 43-5, 50, 53, 63, 65, *65*, 66, *66*, 119, 122, 123, 127
Westernie, The Close 122
Westminster Cathedral 15
Whilome, The Close 42, *42*, 63, 112, 120
Whitefriars, Llanfairfechan 64, 124
Williams, Ralph Vaughan 41
Williams-Ellis, Clough 11, *11*, 73, *73*, 116 *n.4*
Wilson, Henry 9, 16, *17*, 17-20, 25, 76, 87, 99
Windermere 45, 50
windows 11, 29, 31, *46*, 50, 63, 65, 114
    dormer 59-60, *60*
Wirral 50
Witwood 22
Woodard Schools 108
Woodcot, The Close 41-2, 63, 120
workers' housing 11, 72-3, *72-3*
Workington, Cumberland 73, *73*
Wyniat, Llanddulas 125
Wynne, R. O. F. 57